Basic English Grammar
and how to use it

Annette Harrison

First published 2003 by

Macmillan Education Australia under the title *Basic English Grammar*

Reprinted 2007

Third edition (current) published 2014 by HairySun under the title Basic English Grammar

Copyright © Annette Harrison 2003

All rights reserved.
Except under the conditions described in the Copyright Act 1968 of Australia (the Act) and subsequent amendments, no part of this publication may be reproduced, stored in a retrieval system, or transmitted in any form or by any means, electronic, mechanical, photocopying, recording or otherwise, without the prior written permission of the copyright owner.

Educational institutions copying any part of this book for educational purposes under the Act must by covered by a Copyright Agency Limited (CAL) licence for educational institutions and must have given a remuneration notice to CAL.

Licence restrictions must be adhered to. For details of the CAL licence contact:

Copyright Agency Limited, Level 15, 33 Castlereagh Street, Sydney, NSW, 2000
Telephone (02) 9394 7600. Fax (02) 9394 7601. Email: info@copyright.com.au

National Library of Australia cataloguing in publication data

Harrison, Annette, 1945–

    Basic English Grammar.

    Includes index

    ISBN 978 0 9923 0970 1

    1. English language – Grammar

Editor, cover design and text layout: Mike Harrison
Text design: Julie Kirkpatrick

Printed in Australia

Internet addresses
At the time of printing, the internet addresses appearing in this book were correct. Owing to the dynamic nature of the internet, however, we cannot guarantee that all these addresses will remain correct.

CONTENTS

Introduction		1
Author acknowledgments		2
1	**Parts of speech: at a glance**	**3**
	Nouns	4
	Pronouns	4
	Adjectives	5
	Articles	5
	Prepositions	6
	Verbs	7
	Adverbs	7
	Conjunctions	8
	Interjections	8
2	**Parts of speech: explanations and examples**	**9**
	Nouns	10
	Pronouns	14
	Adjectives	22
	Articles	30
	Prepositions	34
	Verbs	38
	Table of the main active verb tenses	45
	List of irregular verbs	73
	Tables of the verb TO BE	77
	Tables of the verb TO HAVE	81
	Tables of the verb TO DO	85
	Adverbs	89
	Conjunctions	96
	Interjections	99
3	**Putting it together**	**100**
	Sentences	100
	Phrases and clauses	103
	Questions in conversation (dialogue)	109
	Direct and indirect (reported) speech	112
	Contractions	114
	Punctuation	117
4	**Making it work and editing it**	**123**
	How does it work?	123
	The rules of editing	136
5	**Major forms of written language**	**137**
	Narrative	137
	Recount	138
	Procedure	139
	Explanation	139
	Exposition	140
	Response	140
	Report	141
	Essay	143
	Glossary	145
	Index	150

INTRODUCTION

Basic English Grammar explores the rules of grammar through easy-to-understand definitions and examples, and then illustrates the practical application of grammar through a series of written exercises. It is an important resource and tool that will assist the reader in all forms of writing, from essays to examinations, job applications, reports and formal letters.

- Chapter 1, 'Parts of speech: at a glance', is a concise overview of the parts of speech, and is a handy and quick reference to the basic rules of grammar.

- Chapter 2, 'Parts of speech: explanations and examples', is an in-depth exploration of parts of speech. Each grammatical point is explained in detail and illustrated with examples. This chapter also includes verbs and verb tenses in table form to demonstrate the relationship between some of the more complex conjugations.

- Chapter 3, 'Putting it together', puts in context the rules of grammar covered in the previous two chapters. The reader is introduced to the formal structures of sentences, phrases and dialogue. In addition, this chapter examines contractions and punctuation.

- Chapter 4, 'Making it work and editing it', demonstrates how to build writing using the rules of grammar. Beginning with a very simple text, this chapter shows how to improve and strengthen the text by adding a series of grammatical elements. In this chapter, ideas are transformed into language through the imaginative use of grammar. This chapter also introduces the principles of editing, including proofreading.

- Chapter 5, 'Major forms of written language', is an overview of the different forms of writing, including narrative, report and essay writing. This chapter contains straightforward descriptions of each writing form, and indicates which parts of speech are most appropriate for each form.

AUTHOR ACKNOWLEDGMENTS

I would like to thank the following people for helping me to produce this book:

- my son Mike for his invaluable help during my TESOL course and editing/producing this new version with me
- my husband John and my daughter Leanne for their encouragement
- my TESOL teachers Kim Greig, Joanne Blaik and Ada de Puit for introducing me to the world of teaching English as a second language
- my ESL students and my English students
- my friend Jan Hallett for her advice on many occasions
- my sister Pat Cooper for her advice and input into this book.

The following resources have been used as reference and resource material in the research and writing of this book:

Eastwood, J. Oxford Practice Grammar, Oxford University Press, 1996

Fletcher, C. Essay Clinic: A Structural Guide to Essay Writing, Macmillan Education Australia, 1997

Murphy, R. English Grammar in Use, Cambridge University Press, 1995

Nesfield, J. Modern English Grammar, The Macmillan Press, London and Basingstoke, 1979

Oshima, A. & Hogue, A. Writing Academic English, Longman, USA, 1991

Rod and Staff English Handbook, Rod and Staff Publishers, Inc., USA, 1983

Thomson, A. & Martinet, A. A Practical English Grammar, Oxford University Press, 1982.

Annette Harrison

CHAPTER 1
PARTS OF SPEECH: AT A GLANCE

Nouns   Articles   Adverbs
Pronouns   Prepositions   Conjunctions
Adjectives   Verbs   Interjections

PARTS OF SPEECH

There are nine Parts of Speech and every word in the English language belongs to at least one Part of Speech. These are the building blocks of Grammar. Each part of speech explains how the word is used. Once you understand how each of these parts of speech work, you can link them together. The following pages give a brief glance at each part of speech.

Nouns - name people or things.

Pronouns - replace or refer to a noun.

Adjectives - describe a noun or a pronoun.

Articles - specify or generalize a noun.

Prepositions - are placed before a noun or pronoun to form a phrase.

Verbs - express action, mood, occurrence, existence and state.

Adverbs - modify verbs, adjectives and other adverbs.

Conjunctions - join words, phrases or clauses in sentences.

Interjections - show strong feelings or emotions.

NOUNS

A noun is a word that names a person or a thing, such as a place, an object, a thought, an emotion or an activity.

USE OF NOUNS

➤ A noun can be the subject in a sentence.

Mary lives in New Zealand.

➤ A noun can be used in the possessive case.

Mary's husband is called Sam.

➤ A noun can be the object in a sentence.

Sam loves *Mary*.

➤ A noun can be singular or plural.

I have a *cat* and two *dogs*.

See Chapter 2, pages 10-13 for further information about nouns.

PRONOUNS

A pronoun is a word that is used instead of a noun (which has already been mentioned) so that it is not necessary to repeat the noun. A pronoun can also replace a noun which is understood or implied.

USE OF PRONOUNS

A pronoun can replace or refer to a noun.

➤ Replacing a noun:

John sent a letter to Annie and *she* thought *it* was funny. (*she* = Annie; *it* = the letter)

➤ Referring to a noun:

The letter, *which* John sent, was very funny. (*which* = the letter)

See Chapter 2, pages 14-21 for further information about pronouns.

ADJECTIVES

An adjective is a word that describes a noun or a pronoun.

USE OF ADJECTIVES

➤ An adjective goes before a noun:

It was a *dark* night. (noun: night)

➤ An adjective goes after some verbs:

Your garden looks *beautiful*. (verb: to look)

➤ Nouns can be used as adjectives:

The *apple* tree. (noun: apple)

➤ An adjective can describe a pronoun:

He is very *tall*. (pronoun: he)

See Chapter 2, pages 22-29 for further information about adjectives.

ARTICLES

An article is a word placed before a noun to specify (qualify) or generalize the noun. There are only three articles: *the, a* and *an*.

USE OF ARTICLES

➤ If we wish to specify a noun, *the* is used:

Can we go to *the* soccer match, please? (a particular match)

Please pass me *the* red apple. (a particular apple)

They said they were going on *the* holiday of a lifetime. (a particular holiday)

➤ If we wish to generalise a noun, *a* or *an* is used:

Can we go to *a soccer match*? (any match)

Please pass me *an apple*. (any apple)

We would love to go on *a* holiday. (any holiday)

Note: The articles are also referred to as determiners. Some adjectives and some pronouns are also referred to as determiners. Determiners limit a noun.

The child is eating *an* ice cream. (articles)

My granddaughter visits me *every* day. (adjectives)

I bought *two* apples and *some* grapes. (adjectives)

Which movie do you want to watch? (adjective)

I want to watch *that* movie with *those* funny cartoons please. (adjectives)

This is a great car. I wouldn't buy *that*. (pronouns)

See Chapter 2, pages 30-33 for further information about articles.

PREPOSITIONS

A preposition is a word that is placed before a noun or a pronoun to form a phrase that shows how one thing is related to another.

USE OF PREPOSITIONS

▶ Prepositions are short words that are usually placed before nouns or pronouns: *to* school, *for* him, *with* them.

Cody enjoys going *to* school.

We bought a new car *for* him.

We loved our holiday *with* them.

▶ Prepositions are words that combine with a noun or pronoun to form a phrase: *in the water, over the bridge, between friends, beside her, by the road.*

The children fell *in the water*.

The cars drove *over the bridge*.

We picked the flowers *by the road*.

▶ When a preposition is placed before a pronoun, the 'object' form of the pronoun is used: *to them, for her, with us.*

We sent a card *to them*.

The man bought the flowers *for her*.

Toni and Gage will come *with us*.

See Chapter 2, pages 34-37 for further information about prepositions.

VERBS

A verb is a word that is used to express action, mood, occurrence or state.

USE OF VERBS

- Verbs are used to say something about a person or a thing.
- Verbs are used to make a statement, ask a question, give a command, make an exclamation or show ownership.
- Verbs are used in tenses – present, past, future and conditional.
- Verbs must agree with the subject in person and number:

    He is a boy.

    They are boys.

See Chapter 2, pages 38-88 for further information about verbs.

ADVERBS

An adverb is a word that modifies some parts of speech but does NOT modify a noun or a pronoun.

USE OF ADVERBS

- Adverbs mainly express how, when, where, how often and how much.

    Pat *carefully* opened the invitation. (how)

    She went to the exhibition *yesterday*. (when)

    The exhibition was held *inside*. (where)

- Adverbs mainly modify a verb, but can also modify an adjective or another adverb.

    He walks *slowly*. (verb: to walk)

    She is a *very* pretty girl. (adjective: pretty)

    The wind blew *quite* suddenly. (adverb: suddenly)

See Chapter 2, pages 89-95 for further information about adverbs.

CONJUNCTIONS

A conjunction is a word that joins words, phrases or clauses in a sentence. Conjunctions are sometimes called linking words or connectors.

USE OF CONJUNCTIONS

➤ A conjunction is used **only** for joining words, phrases or clauses in a sentence.

salt *and* pepper. (words)

in the pool *or* at the beach. (phrases)

Mahira will go to the beach, *but* she will not swim. (clauses)

➤ A conjunction does not qualify a word.

➤ Conjunctions are used to make sentences longer and more interesting.

➤ Some conjunctions can be placed at the beginning of a sentence.

Because I like you, I'll send you an invitation to my party.

Although she didn't know them, she paid for their meal.

See Chapter 2, pages 96-98 for further information about conjunctions.

INTERJECTIONS

An interjection is a word or an exclamation used to show strong feelings or emotions.

USE OF INTERJECTIONS

➤ Interjections are usually involuntary exclamations.

➤ Interjections are usually followed by an exclamation mark: !

➤ Interjections are mainly used in dialogue.

'*Hooray*, we won the cup!' shouted the excited players.

See Chapter 2, page 99 for further information about interjections.

CHAPTER 2
PARTS OF SPEECH: EXPLANATIONS AND EXAMPLES

Nouns

Pronouns

Adjectives

Articles

Prepositions

Verbs:
  Ordinary
  Auxiliary
  Table of main active verb tenses

Verb tenses:
  Present simple
  Present continuous
  Present perfect
  Present perfect continuous
  Past simple
  Past continuous
  Past perfect
  Past perfect continuous
  Future simple
  Future continuous
  Future perfect
  Future perfect continuous

Verbs: modal (auxiliary)

Verbs: passive

Verbs: irregular

Table of verbs *to be*, *to have* and *to do*

Adverbs

Conjunctions

Interjections

Now that you know the nine parts of speech, this chapter explains them in greater detail and they are illustrated with examples.

They are in the same order as in Chapter 1: At a Glance.

This chapter also provides tables of the main active verb tenses, irregular verbs and the verbs *to be*, *to have* and *to do*.

NOUNS

A noun is a word that names a person or a thing, such as a place, an object, a thought, an emotion or an activity.

USE OF NOUNS

➤ A noun can be the subject in a sentence.

Mary lives in New Zealand.

➤ A noun can be used in the possessive case.

Mary's husband is called Sam.

➤ A noun can be the object in a sentence.

Sam loves *Mary*.

➤ Many nouns can be singular or plural. In most cases, to make a noun plural, just add -s.

cat (singular)   cats (plural)

However, there are some other rules for plurals.

a   If a noun ends with *-o* and there is a consonant before the 'o', add *-es*.

potato	potatoes
mango	mangoes
volcano	volcanoes
tomato	tomatoes

b   If a noun ends with *-y* and there is a consonant before the 'y', drop the 'y' and add *-ies*.

pantry	pantries
sentry	sentries
lady	ladies
memory	memories

c   Some nouns that end with *-f* drop the 'f' and add *-ves*.

leaf	leaves
scarf	scarves

Note: Other nouns that end with -f just add -s.

chief	chiefs
cliff	cliffs

d   Some nouns change the vowel.

woman	women
man	men

▶ Some nouns have identical singular and plural forms. In the singular form they take a singular verb and in the plural form they take a plural verb: *sheep, series, aircraft, fish, species*.

sheep	There *is a sheep* in the paddock. (singular)
	There *are some sheep* in the paddock. (plural)
aircraft	That plane *is the biggest aircraft* on the runway. (singular)
	There *are five aircraft* in the hangar. (plural)
fish	There *is a large blue fish* in the aquarium. (singular)
	There *are beautiful fish* on the Great Barrier Reef. (plural)

Note: Use a dictionary if you are not sure how to spell a word.

TYPES OF NOUNS

1 COMMON NOUNS do not refer to one person or thing, but refer to any person or thing of the same kind: *dog, table, man*.

The *dog* walked beside the *man*.

There are two kinds of common nouns.

a   **Count nouns** are nouns that have a singular or plural form: *cow* (singular); *cows* (plural).

I saw a *cow* in that paddock yesterday.

I can see many *cows* there today.

A, an and *one* are only used before singular nouns: *a horse, an apple, one orange*.

These, those, many and numbers greater than one are only used before plural nouns: *these flowers, those trees, many bikes, two cars*.

b   **Mass nouns** or **non-count nouns** are nouns that are neither singular nor plural: *rice, sand, music, money, luck, grass, milk, water, furniture, luggage, housework, transport, homework*.

All the *milk* has spilt on the *grass*.

You cannot use *a* or a number before a mass noun: *a* money and *three* sand are both wrong.

Words such as *the*, *my* and *his* or *her* are used before count or mass nouns: *the book, my shoes, his money, her car.*

This and *that* are used before singular or mass nouns: *this house, that milk.*

Some and *any* are used before plural or mass nouns: *some apples, any rice.*

2 **PROPER NOUNS** always have a capital letter and refer to one particular person or thing: *Tom, Jeanie, England, Australia, Mr Jones.*

Jeanie went to *Canada*.

3 **ABSTRACT NOUNS** refer to some quality, state or action.

a **Quality**: *beauty, loveliness, height, courage, hope, joy, love, humility, sympathy, kindness, colour, justice.*

There is great *joy* when a baby is born.

b **State**: *youth, manhood, poverty, greatness, freedom, authority, equality, pleasure, life, death.*

There is little hope in *poverty*.

c **Action**: *movement, laughter, fear, flight, revenge, judgment, choice.*

Laughter is the best medicine.

4 **COLLECTIVE NOUNS** refer to a group or collection of similar things: *team, crowd, flock, group, family, swarm, parliament.*

The *family* watched the *team* play.

5 **GERUNDS** (sometimes called Verbals – see note on page 43) are 'ing' words that are formed from verbs but are used as nouns: *skiing, swimming, studying, reading, walking, gardening, shopping, eating, working, going, taking, winning.*

Skiing and *swimming* are my favourite sports.

Gerunds can be used as the subject, object or complement of a sentence.

Working is an essential part of life. (subject)

Monica loves *dancing*. (object)

Nate is interested in *going* overseas. (complement)

6 **COMPOUND NOUNS** occur when nouns are joined together to make another word: *armchair, bookcase, hairbrush, handbag.*

I found my *hairbrush* on the *bookcase*.

Compound nouns don't need to be joined together: *birthday card, light switch, coat hanger, table cloth*.

Note: The first noun is often called an adjective. See 'Use of adjectives' on page 5 and page 22.

The last word is usually made into the plural form: *birthday cards, coat hangers, table cloths*.

NOUN PHRASES AND NOUN CLAUSES

➤ **Noun phrases** are a group of words containing a noun, without a verb.

Wendy and David have remodelled *the bathroom*.

This car will be very useful.

➤ **Noun clauses** are dependent clauses that do the work of a noun, contain a verb and can be the subject, object or complement to a verb.

<u>What she did</u> was very wrong. (subject)

They decided <u>that she was right</u>. (object)

The film was exactly <u>what we expected</u>. (complement)

Examples of different types of nouns in sentences

The *cats* sat on a *table*. (common – count)

I have two *sons* and a *daughter*. (common – count)

A *dog* ran after the *car*. (common – count)

We saw some *horses* in the *paddock*. (common – count)

David only drinks *water* or *milk*. (common – mass)

Most people dislike *housework*. (common – mass)

Myung Ho and *Eun Sook* went back to *South Korea*. (proper)

Leanne and *Mark* went to *Vietnam*. (proper)

Beauty is in the eye of the beholder. (abstract)

Laughter is the best medicine. (abstract)

My friend is in *Parliament*. (collective)

The *family* went on holiday. (collective)

Sleeping, *eating* and *reading* are my favourite pastimes. (gerund)

Flying is not my favourite pastime. (gerund)

I bought a new *light bulb* to put in my *table lamp*. (compound)

We took our lunch in a *plastic bag*. (compound)

PRONOUNS

A pronoun is a word that is used instead of a noun (which has already been mentioned) so that it is not necessary to repeat the noun. A pronoun can also replace a noun which is understood or implied.

USE OF PRONOUNS

A pronoun replaces or refers to a noun.

➤ Replacing a noun:

John sent a letter to Annie and *she* thought *it* was funny. (*she* = Annie; *it* = the letter)

➤ Referring to a noun:

The letter, *which* John sent, was very funny. (*which* = the letter)

TYPES OF PRONOUNS

1 PERSONAL PRONOUNS

Personal pronouns refer to the person/s speaking, the person/s or thing/s spoken to, and the person/s or thing/s spoken about.

➤ **Singular**: *I/me, you, he/him, she/her, it*

She is a famous movie star and is married to *him*.

➤ **Plural**: *we/us, you, they/them*

We drove home and a car followed *us*.

TABLE 2.1 Personal pronouns

	Subject	Object	
Singular			
First person	I	me	The speaker
Second person	you	you	The person or thing being spoken to
Third person	he, she, it	him, her, it	The person or thing being spoken about
Plural			
First person	we	us	The speaker and others being spoken for
Second person	you	you	More than one person or thing spoken to
Third person	they	them	More than one person or thing spoken about

Examples of personal pronouns in sentences:

I am going to Sydney next week. (*I* is the subject, singular, first person)

You can come too, Leanne. (*You* is the subject, singular, second person)

She will drive to Sydney. (*She* is the subject, singular, third person)

John will come with *me*. (*me* is the object, singular, first person)

Will he go with *you*, Annie? (*you* is the object, singular, second person)

Annie will go with *him*. (*him* is the object, singular, third person)

We will travel together. (*We* is the subject, plural, first person)

You will both go with Mark. (*You* is the subject, plural, second person)

They will stay at home. (*They* is the subject, plural, third person)

Jade can come with *us*. (*us* is the object, plural, first person)

Maisy can go with *you* two. (*you* is the object, plural, second person)

We will drive with *them*. (*them* is the object, plural, third person)

A basic dialogue showing personal pronouns:

Pat:	Have *you* been in that new shop, Anne? (*you* = Anne)
Anne:	No, *I* haven't. (*I* = Anne)
Pat:	Oh, *it's* good. There was a dress in that shop and *it* wasn't very expensive. (first *it* = shop; second *it* = dress)
Anne:	Leanne bought some pants there and *she* said that *they* were lovely. (*she* = Leanne; *they* = pants)
Pat:	*We* should go there together. (*We* = Pat and Anne)
Anne:	Yes, please come with *me*. (*me* = Anne)
Pat:	Let's take Michelle and Sue with *us*. (*us* = Pat and Anne)
Anne:	Yes, *they* would love it. (*they* = Michelle and Sue)
Pat:	Paul thought *he* would go. (*he* = Paul)
Anne:	I don't know *him*. (*him* = Paul)
Pat:	Oh, Paul likes Betty. Do you know *her*? (*her* = Betty)
Anne:	I don't know either of *them*. (*them* = Paul and Betty)

2 **POSSESSIVE PRONOUNS** are pronouns that replace possessive adjectives (or possessive determiners) and still show that something belongs to somebody: *mine, yours, his, hers, ours, yours, theirs.*

A friend of *mine* is visiting Rome.

That small house is *ours*.

Note: Possessive adjectives – *my, your, his, her, its, our, your, their* – look like possessive pronouns, but are actually adjectives, which go before a noun and show possession.

My friend is visiting Rome. (possessive adjective plus a noun)

Our house is very small. (possessive adjective plus a noun)

Examples of possessive pronouns:

Where is Wendy? This coat is *hers*. (her coat)

Hello David. Is this hat *yours*? (your hat)

A basic dialogue showing how to use possessive pronouns and possessive adjectives:

Anne:	Michelle and Jaime want us to go to *their* house. (possessive adjective)
Pat:	OK. Would you like me to drive *my* car? (possessive adjective)
Anne:	No thanks, we can go in *mine*. (possessive pronoun)
Pat:	I thought *yours* was being fixed. (possessive pronoun)
Anne:	There was a noise in *its* engine, but it's OK now. (possessive adjective)
Pat:	Wait until you see *theirs*. It's brand new. (possessive pronoun)

3 **REFLEXIVE AND EMPHATIC PRONOUNS** refer to the subject.

TABLE 2.2 Reflexive and emphatic pronouns

	Singular	Plural
First person	myself	ourselves
Second person	yourself	yourselves
Third person	himself, herself, itself	themselves

➤ **Reflexive pronouns** refer to the subject.

Jane will make *herself* a sandwich. (referring to Jane)

Examples showing the person, singular and plural:

I will drive *myself* to the shops. (*myself* is singular, first person)

You can make *yourself* a drink. (*yourself* is singular, second person)

Jan drove *herself* to work. (*herself* is singular, third person)

We can entertain *ourselves*. (*ourselves* is plural, first person)

You can play by *yourselves*. (*yourselves* is plural, second person)

They played by *themselves* all day. (*themselves* is plural, third person)

Here are some more examples:

I am going to France next year, so I'm teaching *myself* French.

The girl jumped off the wall and hurt *herself*.

You won the tennis competition. You must be proud of *yourself*.

The children were sick and were feeling sorry for *themselves*.

My iron switches *itself* off after eight minutes.

We have money so we can pay for the tickets *ourselves*.

John can make *himself* a cup of coffee.

You all played well. You should be proud of *yourselves*.

➤ **Emphatic pronouns** are similar to reflexive pronouns, but with a different meaning. They put the stress on self.

I'm writing the book *myself*. (without any help)

The Queen *herself* drove the car. (not her driver)

Here are some more examples:

I made this cake *myself*.

I knew you were going to Paris. You told me *yourself*.

The Pope *himself* welcomed the children.

The Prime Minister *herself* changed the tyre on her vehicle.

The restaurant *itself* was awful, but the food was delicious.

We painted the house *ourselves*.

Did you children write this book *yourselves*?

The apartment *itself* is large, but the bedrooms are too small.

4 RELATIVE PRONOUNS are used to introduce relative (adjective) clauses and refer or relate to people or things: *who, whom, whose, which, that.*

➤ *who* refers only to people – singular and plural.

➤ *whom* refers only to people – singular and plural.

➤ *whose* shows possession and refers to people or things – singular and plural.

➤ *which* refers to things – singular and plural.

➤ *that* refers to things or people – singular and plural.

The girl *who* was singing was my sister.

Marie, *whom* everyone liked, played the piano beautifully.

I rang my friend, *whose* son was going overseas.

I dislike loud music, *which* gives me a headache.

It was the best movie *that* we ever saw.

These clauses are called **relative (adjective) clauses**. There are three types:

a **Defining relative (adjective) clauses** begin with *who* or *that*.

The man *who* was shouting was my father.

It was the best movie *that* we had seen.

There are no commas to isolate the clause from the rest of the sentence because the clause is needed to give clear understanding of the noun – e.g. *man*.

b **Non-defining relative (adjective) clauses** begin with *who*, *whom* or *whose*.

Paul, *who* had been travelling all day, wanted to stop for a rest.

Marie, *whom* everyone liked, played the piano beautifully.

Annie, *whose* foot was sprained, had trouble walking.

Commas are used to isolate the clause from the rest of the sentence, as it is not necessary to give clear understanding to the noun – e.g. *Paul*.

c **Connective relative (adjective) clauses** begin with *who, whom, whose* or *which*.

Mike met Paul, *who* offered him a job.

The Queen has three sons, one of *whom* will be King one day.

I rang my friend, *whose* son was going overseas.

I dislike loud music, *which* gives me a headache.

Commas are used to isolate the clause from the rest of the sentence, as it is not necessary to give clear understanding to the noun. These clauses are similar to non-defining relative (adjective) clauses, but are usually placed after the object of the main active verb – e.g. *Paul*.

5 **DEMONSTRATIVE PRONOUNS** replace the noun if the meaning is clear: *this, these, that, those, one, ones, none.*

Look at my new pen. I bought *this* yesterday.

➤ *This* and *these* are used for things near the speaker.

➤ *That* and *those* are used for things further away from the speaker.

What do you think about my new dress? I bought *this* yesterday. (dress)

What do you think about my new dresses? I bought *these* yesterday. (dresses)

Look at the shirt over there. I bought *that* yesterday. (shirt)

Look at the shirts over there. I bought *those* yesterday. (shirts)

Sue ate an ice-cream. Michelle didn't want *one*. (ice-cream)

There were three full bins. There were three empty *ones*. (bins)

David had some money. Wendy had *none*. (money)

6 **INTERROGATIVE PRONOUNS** ask questions: *who, whom, whose, what, which.*

➤ For people we use:

a **who** (subject)

Who took my keys? (who: subject) *Leanne* took them.

b **who** or **whom** (object)

Who/whom did you meet? (who/whom: object) I met *Mark*.

c **whose** (possession).

Whose are these? (whose: possession) They are *Jade's*.

➤ For things we use *what* (subject and object).

What kept you? (what: subject) The *traffic* was heavy.

What did he drink? (what: object) He drank a *cup of coffee*.

➤ For people or things, when we want to make a choice we use *which* (subject and object).

Which of them is the youngest? (which: subject) *Mike* is the youngest.

Which do you like best? (which: object) I like this *book* best.

7 INDEFINITE PRONOUNS do not replace a noun previously mentioned, but replace a noun that is understood or implied.

Everyone stood for the National Anthem.

Indefinite pronouns include: *someone, somebody, something, somewhere, anyone, anybody, anything, anywhere, everyone, everybody, everything, no-one, nobody, nowhere, one, another, others, each, some, none.*

Someone stole my car.

Is this *somebody's* seat?

Something was wrong with the dog.

My neighbours have gone *somewhere*.

Does *anyone* know the time?

Would *anybody* like a ticket?

Do you want *anything* from the shops?

You can go *anywhere* you like.

Everyone was ready to leave.

Everybody was in the car.

Everything has been stolen.

No-one has ever been kind to me.

Nobody loves me.

They went *nowhere*.

At times like this, *one* does one's best.

He won't marry her. He loves *another*.

Others have left this mess.

Each to his own.

Some will always agree.

None can change the future.

PRONOUN CLAUSES

Relative pronouns are used to introduce relative (adjective) clauses, which refer or relate to people or things: *who, whom, whose, which, that.*

There are three types of relative (adjective) clauses.

1 **Defining relative (adjective) clauses** begin with *who* or *that.*

   The girl *who was singing* was my sister.

   It was the best movie *that we ever saw*.

There are no commas to isolate the clause from the rest of the sentence because the clause is needed to give clear understanding of the noun: e.g. *girl*.

2 **Non-defining relative (adjective) clauses** begin with *who, whom* or *whose.*

   Jade, *who had been sleeping all morning,* was very thirsty.

   Marie, *whom everyone liked*, played the piano beautifully.

   Annie, *whose foot was broken*, had trouble walking.

Commas are used to isolate the clause from the rest of the sentence, as it is not necessary to give clear understanding to the noun – e.g. *Jade.*

3 **Connective relative (adjective) clauses** begin with *who, whom, whose* or *which*.

   Paul married Katie, *who worked with Mike*.

   The Queen has three sons, *one of whom will be King one day*.

   I rang my friend, *whose son was going overseas*.

   I dislike loud music, *which gives me a headache*.

Commas are used to isolate the clause from the rest of the sentence, as it is not necessary to give clear understanding to the noun. These clauses are similar to non-defining relative (adjective) clauses, but are usually placed after the object of the main, active verb, e.g. *Katie.*

ADJECTIVES

An adjective is a word that describes a noun or a pronoun.

USE OF ADJECTIVES

➤ An adjective goes before a noun.

You have a *beautiful* garden. (noun: garden)

It was a *dark* night. (noun: night)

➤ An adjective goes after some verbs.

The bride looks *stunning*. (verb: to look)

The crowd became *angry*. (verb: to become)

The main verbs that go with adjectives are:

to be:	Your garden is *beautiful*.
to appear:	The sky appears *red*.
to become:	He had become *angry*.
to taste:	The milk tasted *sour*.
to smell:	The dinner smelt *wonderful*.
to seem:	The room seemed *large*.
to get:	It was getting *dark*.
to stay:	The day stayed *warm*.
to look:	The child looked *tired*.
to feel:	I felt *cold*.

➤ Nouns can be used as adjectives.

The *apple* tree is near the fence. (noun: apple)

Aili sent Jan a *birthday* card. (noun: birthday)

➤ An adjective can describe a pronoun.

He is very *tall*. (pronoun: he)

She was *happy*. (pronoun: she)

TYPES OF ADJECTIVES

1. **Descriptive (general)**: *pretty* girl, *big* boat, *round* ball, *red* nose.

    The *pretty* girl threw the *big*, *round* ball into the water.

2. **Comparative (comparing)**: *darker* shade, *cheaper* book, *more useful* map.

    Atsuko decided to buy the *darker* shade of blue to paint her bedroom wall.

3. **Superlative (highest/lowest degree)**: *darkest* shade, *cheapest* book, *most useful* map.

    Yumiko and her family stayed in the *cheapest* hotel.

4. **Quantitative (how many?)** - also known as determiners: *one* book, *two* boys, *some* students.

    Some students couldn't work because they only had *one* book between them.

5. **Interrogative (asking)** – also known as determiners: *which* book? *what* ideas?

    Which book did you buy?

6. **Demonstrative (noun referred to):** - also known as determiners: *this* book, *that* girl, *these* boys, *those* children.

    Those children should not be playing near *that* road.

7. **Distributive (referring to each one)** – also known as determiners: *each* day, *every* child, *either/neither* day.

    Every child in the world needs love.

8. **Possessive (ownership)** – also known as determiners: *my* hat, *your* bike, *his* dog, *her* car, *its* bone, *our* house, *your* wife, *their* boat.

    He left *his* hat in *their* boat.

ADJECTIVE PHRASES AND CLAUSES

Adjective phrases contain a group of words without a verb, which describe something.

   Yuki is the lady <u>with dark hair</u>.

Adjective clauses (relative clauses) are dependent clauses (dependent clause = a group of words with a verb), which are introduced by a relative pronoun or a relative adverb. They describe or modify a noun or pronoun in the independent clause. Adjective (relative) clauses are placed directly after the noun or pronoun that they describe or modify.

- **Relative pronouns**: *who, whom, whose, which* and *that*

    James wanted the job *that* was in Hong Kong.

    He didn't know anyone *who* lived in Hong Kong.

    James, *to whom I was speaking*, told me about his job.

    Carmelita, *whose* husband James was overseas, flew out to meet him.

    She didn't like the plane trip, *which* was very long.

- **Relative adverbs**: *where, when* and *why*

    Carmelita hadn't been to the flat *where* James lived.

    August, *when they went*, was very cold.

    They told us the reason *why* they went away.

There are three types of adjective or relative clauses.

1 **Defining adjective/relative clauses**:

    The girl *who served us* is no longer in that shop.

    The pool *that we swam in* was huge.

    Carmelita hadn't been to the flat *where James lived*.

    They told us the reasons *why they went away.*

There are no commas to isolate the clause from the rest of the sentence because the clause is needed to give a clear understanding of the noun – e.g. *girl*.

2 **Non-defining adjective/relative clauses**:

    Aili, *who went to Russia,* bought this brooch for me.

    Jackie, *to whom I was speaking,* suddenly fainted.

    Jill, *whose daughter was overseas*, showed me photos of the family.

    August, *when I was sick,* was very cold.

Commas are used to isolate the clause from the rest of the sentence, as the clause is not necessary to give a clear understanding of the noun – e.g. *Aili*.

3 **Connective adjective/relative clauses**:

    Felicity rang Julie, *who then rang me*.

    Our friend had triplets, *two of whom were boys*.

    We went to visit Julie, *whose children were at home*.

Commas are used to isolate the clause from the rest of the sentence, as the clause is not necessary to give a clear understanding of the noun. These clauses are similar to non-defining adjective/relative clauses, but are usually placed after the object of the main, active verb – e.g. *Julie*.

-ING AND -ED

Adjectives ending in *-ing* are known as present participles. Those ending in *-ed* are known as past participles. Participles are sometimes called verbals (see note on page 43).

Look at these two words: *interesting* and *interested*. Both of these words are adjectives.

➤ When an adjective ends with *-ing* it describes something and the effect it has on somebody.

   They found the book very *interesting*.

➤ When an adjective ends with *-ed* it describes how a person or living thing feels.

   I am really *interested* in this book, too.

More examples:

They won a prize. The people were very *excited*. (how they felt)

Leanne goes whale watching. She's *interested* in whales. (how she feels)

I love watching documentaries. I think they are *fascinating*. (what they are like)

I have lost the map. Now I am *confused*. (how I feel)

It was winter, so the amount of sunshine was *surprising*. (the effect it had)

I thought the car was going to crash and I was *terrified*. (how I felt)

The house was old and *depressing*. (what it was like)

The father told the children an *amusing* story. (what it was like)

The movie was *boring* and we were *annoyed* that we went. (what it was like and how we felt)

Paul was *tired* and found the spa bath *relaxing*. (how he felt and what it was like)

See Chapter 3, page 104 for participle phrases.

Sentences showing both –ing and –ed adjectives:

It was *disappointing* to miss our friends. Everyone was *disappointed*.

We watched a *frightening* movie. The children especially were *frightened*.

The judges' decision was *puzzling*. The competitors were *puzzled* by the decision.

Congratulations, what *thrilling* news! You must be *thrilled*.

The trip was great, but *exhausting*. We were *exhausted* when we arrived home.

The news about the volcanic eruption was *shocking*. We were all *shocked*.

The animation in the film was *amazing*. The audience was *amazed*.

POSITION OF GENERAL DESCRIPTIVE ADJECTIVES

When more than one adjective is used before a noun there is usually a correct order, as is shown in the numbered list below. The adjectives are separated with a comma.

She has a *new, red, silk* dress.

1 **Quality** (how good/bad is it?): *awful, nice, beautiful, wonderful*

   It was a *wonderful* party.

2 **Size** (how big is it?): *big, tall, small, short*

   She is a very *short* girl.

3 **Age** (how old is it?): *new, old, young*

   He is only a *young* child.

4 **Shape** (what is its shape?): *cubic, square, oval, rectangular, round*

   They threw the *round* ball.

5 **Colour** (what is its colour?): *green, brown, blue, red*

   I like the *red* balloon.

6 **Origin** (where is it from?): *Australian, Thai, Finnish, Japanese*

   I know a *Japanese* student.

7 **Type** (what type is it?): *checked, blossom, lacy, embroidered, frilled*.

   Yumiko sat under the *blossom* tree.

8 **Composition/material** (what is it made of?): *plastic, wooden, cotton, silk*

   Lucie wore the *silk* dress.

9 **Purpose** (what is it for?): *dining, washing*

   Heejin has a *washing* machine.

This is how we can use more than one adjective:

   I have a *new, green* dress. (age comes before colour)

We can even be silly:

   A *beautiful, big, old, round, brown, English, wooden, dining* table.

   Note: If, however, there are two adjectives of colour, they are separated by 'and'. For more than two adjectives, use commas and 'and' before the last adjective.

   Stuart has a *blue and white* shirt.

   A *red, white and blue* logo was on the handout.

SOME MORE GENERAL DESCRIPTIVE ADJECTIVES

(There are more examples, these are just a few to get you started)

1 QUALITY (how good/bad is it?):

noisy	quiet	warm	cold
expensive	cheap	loud	gentle
hot	chilly	dear	inexpensive
beautiful	handsome	pretty	elegant
peaceful	ugly	exquisite	lavish
cute	wonderful	bright	messy
outrageous	delicious	awful	nice

2 SIZE (how big is it?):

huge	large	big	tall
short	small	long	massive
tiny	little	enormous	wide
thin	thick	narrow	gigantic
slender	plump	fat	extensive

3 AGE (how old is it?):

old	new	young	ancient
modern	fresh	immature	current
antiquated	recent	fashionable	advanced

4 SHAPE (what is its shape?):

| round | square | oval | circular |
| rectangular | oblong | octagonal | triangular |

5 COLOUR (what is its colour?):

red	blue	yellow	green
orange	pink	brown	black
white	purple	mauve	gold
silver	violet	olive	beige

6 ORIGIN (where is it from?):

Australian	English	Finnish	Japanese
Thai	Korean	American	Canadian
African	Egyptian	Russian	European

7 TYPE (what type is it?):

striped	checked	floral	patterned
printed	plain	embroidered	qulited

8 COMPOSITION/MATERIAL (what is it made of?):

plastic	wooden	cotton	silk
glass	brick	polyester	chocolate
woollen	metal	leather	concrete

9 PURPOSE (what is it for?):

washing (machine)	swimming (pool)	gardening (book)	dining (table)

Examples of more than one adjective put into order

- Vase: *what, wooden, tall, beautiful*:
  What beautiful, tall, wooden vase?

- Mirrors: *those, round, small, cheaper*:
  Those cheaper, small, round mirrors.

- Table: *this, wooden, magnificent, large, dining, old*:
  This magnificent, large, old, wooden, dining table.

- Chair: *his, lounge, leather, new, comfortable*:
  His comfortable, new, leather, lounge chair.

- Mat: *one, cotton, round, colourful*:
  One round, colourful, cotton mat.

- Girl: *which, Finnish, young, attractive, tall*:
  Which attractive, tall, young, Finnish girl?

The adjectives in this basic text are in italics:

The *young* girl was very *excited*. She had arrived at the home of the *famous* author. She was hoping to be offered the *best* job in the world.

The home was *beautiful* and the garden was *exquisite* with *spring* blooms. There were *two* fountains and a *stone* statue in the middle of the *circular* driveway.

She knocked on the *front* door and a woman opened it. The girl recognized the author immediately, but she was *taller* than her photos, with very *blue* eyes.

The interview was conducted in a *sunny* room where the author worked. On her desk was an *antique* vase filled with *yellow*, *white* and *pink* peonies. The *darkest*, *pink* peonies were *glorious*. The girl wished that she could take some of the flowers home to *her* mother. She also hoped that she would be working in *this* room *every* day.

Here is a dialogue showing how to use *adjectives*.

This family is living and working in Peru at the moment and are talking about what they like about Peru.

Alison I love Peru. *Great* food, *warm* culture and *wonderful* friends.

Daniel I like *my* friends. I like playing with them, especially tennis. I also have an *awesome drum* teacher and I love playing loudly on *my* drums.

Heidi Well, *my* friends are *amazing*. They wear *colourful* clothes and I love *their* ponchos and *their* beanies with *long* tassels on top and on the sides.

Elena I think Peru is an *interesting* country with snow on the *huge* mountains. I can speak Spanish with *our* friends.

Stuart I enjoy running with *some* friends. When we meet, Mum reckons all she hears is *raucous* laughter.

Heidi I like Trujillo. I love riding horses and cooking. I also enjoy tennis and I can beat all the boys in *my* class now. It's *fun*.

Elena *My favourite* things are swimming, riding, reading and playing *my* keyboard.

Daniel What about *our terrific* holiday recently? I enjoyed cycling and fishing.

Stuart I think *our* most *exciting* experience here in Peru was sliding down the *enormous sand* dunes.

Alison I think the *best* experience I've had was going to *ancient* Machu Picchu. It was *incredible*.

ARTICLES

An article is a word placed before a noun to specify (qualify) or generalize the noun. There are only three articles: *the*, *a* and *an*. *The* qualifies a noun and *a* and *an* generalize a noun.

USE OF THE ARTICLES

➤ If we wish to specify a noun, *the* is used.

Can we go to *the soccer match*, please? (a particular match)

Please pass me *the* red apple. (a particular apple)

They said they were going on *the* holiday of a lifetime. (a particular holiday)

➤ If we wish to generalise a noun, *a* or *an* is used.

Can we go to *a soccer match*? (any match)

Please pass me *an apple*. (any apple)

We would love to go on *a* holiday. (any holiday)

Notes

1 *The* is the root form of *this*, *that*, *these* and *those*, which are adjectives and always refer to a specific thing or things.
2 *A* and *an* are abbreviations of *one*, which is an adjective and always refers to a general thing. The articles are, in fact, adjectives.
3 The articles are also referred to as *determiners*. Some adjectives and some pronouns are also referred to as *determiners*. *Determiners* limit a noun.

The child is eating *an* ice cream. (articles)

My granddaughter visits me *every* day. (adjectives)

I bought *two* apples and *some* grapes. (adjectives)

Which movie do you want to watch? (adjective)

I want to watch *that* movie with *those* funny cartoons please. (adjectives)

This is a great car. I wouldn't buy *that*. (pronouns)

TYPES OF ARTICLES

1 THE DEFINITE ARTICLE: *THE*

The is placed before singular or plural nouns that we wish to qualify: *the* book, *the* books; *the* boy, *the* boys; *the* girl, *the* girls.

The is pronounced differently before nouns beginning with vowels and before nouns beginning with consonants.

- *The* is pronounced (sounds like) *Thee* before nouns beginning with vowels:

  The (thee) apple, the (thee) eggs, the (thee) igloo, the (thee) onion, the (thee) unicorn.

- *The* is pronounced (sounds like) *th'* before nouns beginning with consonants:

  Th' book, th' candle, th' kettle, th' music, th' students, th' wood.

The use of the definite article

- Before some nouns that are singular and represent only one of a kind:

  the sun, *the* moon, *the* earth, *the* Prime Minister of Australia.

- Before some nouns that have already been referred to:

  John bought a new computer yesterday. *The computer* is excellent.

- Before a noun when it is clear that it is referring to a particular thing:

  The children are in *the pool* in my backyard. (my particular pool)

  Hop in *the car* and we'll go home. (a particular car)

- Before a musical instrument:

  Mike plays *the* piano and *the* violin.

- Before mass nouns:

  Aidan plays in *the* team.

- Before some proper nouns:

  the Prime Minister, *the* Nullarbor Plain, *the* Queen

2 THE INDEFINITE ARTICLE: *A* AND *AN*

A and *an* are placed before singular nouns that we wish to generalise: *a* table, *an* uncle.

- *A* is placed before a word starting with a consonant or a vowel that is pronounced like a consonant: *a* book, *a* girl, *a* unicorn.

- *An* is placed before a word starting with a vowel and some words that start with 'h': *an* animal, *an* egg, *an* igloo, *an* orange, *an* umbrella, *an* honoured guest.

The use of the indefinite article

➤ Before a count noun that is singular when it is mentioned for the first time:

We need *a drink*.

Leanne has *a* great *job*.

Jade likes to eat *an apple*.

➤ Before a count noun that is singular, but includes a number of people or things:

A family needs love.

A school must have teachers.

An audience enjoys a good performance.

➤ Before an occupation:

Nina is *a mother*, *a grandmother*, and *a great grandmother*.

John is *a pilot*.

Mark is *an artist*.

➤ Before some numbers, sizes, prices, speeds, measurements, and so on: *a* **dozen**, *an* inch, *a* million, *a* kilo, $10 *a* metre, ten miles *an* hour

They cost $5 *a* dozen.

If you give him *an* inch, he'll take *a* mile.

What would we do with *a* million dollars?

I have put on *a* kilo and I need to diet.

They said it would be $10 *a* metre.

We had to drive ten miles *an* hour.

➤ Before a count noun when something is emphasized:

What *a* great *party*!

What *an* interesting *country*!

What *a* fabulous experience!

SOME EXAMPLES USING *THE*, *A* AND *AN*

The

Look at *the moon*. (singular noun and only one moon)

Michelle lives in *the country* (as opposed to the city).

Can I have *the* red *pen* over there on that table please? (a particular pen)

James flew to *the Caribbean*. (only one Caribbean and a proper noun)

That man playing *the guitar* is my friend. (musical instrument)

The weather was really bad yesterday. (mass noun and only one of a kind)

We bought some fish. *The fish* was delicious. (noun already referred to)

A and an

Rosie is tired. She needs *a sleep*. (singular count noun mentioned for the first time)

Sue is *a* great *mother*. (occupation)

Wendy has *a* beautiful *home*. (singular count noun mentioned for the first time)

Mark is *an accountant*. (occupation)

Jaime is *a farmer* and *a carpenter*. (occupations)

There were *a dozen cakes* in the box. (number)

A baby is *a* precious *gift*. (singular count noun but includes many)

We walked for *a kilometre*. (measurement)

David is *an artist*. (occupation)

Give her *an inch* and she'll take *a mile*. (measurement)

What *a* fabulous *place*! (count noun emphasised)

Combinations of the, a and an

Aidan ate *an apple* while he watched *the snow* falling.

Pat goes to *the pool* for *a swim*.

Nina goes to *the shops* in *a car*.

Jack built *a house* in *the country*.

John works in *the city* in *a* large *office*.

Cody played in *a* great *team* in *the final*.

Timothy's Dad is *an accountant* and plays *the guitar*.

An orchestra must have *the* best *instruments*.

PREPOSITIONS

A preposition is a word that is placed before a noun or a pronoun to form a phrase that shows how one thing is related to another.

USE OF PREPOSITIONS

➤ Prepositions are short words that are usually placed before nouns or pronouns: *to* school, *for* him, *with* them.

We bought a new car *for* him.

➤ Prepositions are words that combine with a noun or pronoun to form a phrase: *in the water, over the bridge, between friends, beside her, by the road.*

The children fell *in the water*.

➤ When a preposition is placed before a pronoun, the 'object' form of the pronoun is used: *to them, for her, with us*.

The man bought the flowers *for her.*

TYPES OF PREPOSITIONS

Prepositions show relationship, including time, place, instrument and cause.

➤ **Time**: *in* February, *on* 22 March, *at* lunchtime.

My birthday is *in* February.

➤ **Place**: *under* the bridge, *on* the chair, *beside* the car.

The children ran *under* the bridge.

➤ **Instrument**: *with* a knife, *without* a hat, *by* the hand.

He cut himself *with* a knife.

I went to the beach *without* my hat.

She took the child *by* the hand.

➤ **Cause**: *for* him, talking *about*, die *of*.

She bought it *for* him.

What is he talking *about*?

What did she die *of*?

Although there are a number of different types of prepositions, the main two show time and place.

- **Prepositions of time**: *after, at, by, during, for, from, in, on, since, till, to, until.*

    Lexi will be in Jordan *by* the end of July.

    She can write her report *during* the flight.

    Leonie is going to Indonesia *for* nine days.

    She will be teaching *from* Monday *to* Friday.

    Steve hasn't travelled to Indonesia *since* 2010.

    They will stay in the airport *till/until* their hosts arrive.

    Johno will be in Western Australia *in* October.

    He will be with his family *at* Christmas.

    Marilyn and John will rest *after* their holiday.

- **Prepositions of place**: *about, above, across, along, among, around, at, away from, behind, below, beneath, beside, between, beyond, by, down, from, in, inside, in/into, in front of, near, next to, off, on, on/onto, on top of, opposite, out of, outside, over, past, round, through, to, towards, under, up, with.*

    There is a big sign *above* the counter *in* that shop.

    They stopped *at* the lights and then went *across* the road.

    They walked *past* the park and *along* the main road.

    Kylie and her dog ran *out of* the gate and *around* the block.

    The racquets are *behind* the tennis balls *on* that shelf.

    His graduation gown was long and was *below* his knees.

    He walked *beneath* the beautiful trees.

    Sue sat *beside* Rosie *in* the movie theatre.

    They swam safely *between* the flags.

    Maisy went *down* the steps *to* the car park.

    Lauren bought a pie *from* the bakery and Tim put it *into* the oven.

    Look, there is a new sign *in front of* the store.

    We lost the house key, so we couldn't get *inside* the house.

    The children put a flag *on top of* the sandcastle.

    I think the travel books are *opposite* the history section, *next to* the biographies.

    I waited *outside* the bank until it opened.

    The thief jumped *over* the wall as Bev walked *through* the back door.

    Why is Bill walking *towards* those shops?

    There was dust *under* the bed.

    The cat was stuck *up* a tree.

▶ Prepositions of time and place: in, on and at are three words that can be used to describe a time or a place.

a Time:

in	We flew to Singapore *in* 1995.
on	We arrived *on* Wednesday.
at	We landed *at* seven-thirty.

In is used for some time in a day, a week or longer.

The baby sleeps *in* the afternoon.

We visit Grandma *in* the school holidays.

I wonder what will happen *in* the next three months.

In is used for a month, a year or a season.

The football finals were held *in* September.

Woo Sun went to Turkey *in* 2000.

We go to the beach *in* summer.

On is used for a day or a date.

We go to church *on* Sunday.

I love reading a book *on* a rainy day.

Our anniversary is *on* 22 March.

On is used for a particular day.

These photos were taken *on* our wedding day.

On Christmas Day we open our gifts.

At is used for a specific time on the clock or an event.

They finish work *at* 5pm.

We eat muesli *at* breakfast time.

Tim was in school *at* that point in time.

At is used for a period of a few days.

The family gets together *at* Christmas.

We always relax *at* the end of the week.

b Place:

in	Tom swam *in* the pool.
on	Carrie sat *on* the kitchen stool.
at	Zoe and Noah were standing *at* the door.

In is used when something is surrounded on all sides.

Lucie was swimming *in* our pool.

May was playing *in* the playpen.

John was shaving *in* the bathroom.

In is used for a street, village, town, city or country.

Our new house is *in* Kent Road.

We stayed with Bernie and Eth *in* Maidenhead.

They saw the Roman Colosseum *in* Rome.

On is used for a surface.

The baby crawled *on* the floor.

What is written *on* your T-shirt?

The astronauts landed *on* the moon.

On is used for a road, river or border.

He loves travelling *on* a country road.

We rowed our boat *on* the river.

They lived *on* the border of Queensland and New South Wales.

At is used for a position.

She was waiting *at* the door.

We stopped the car *at* the lights.

We met each day *at* the bus stop.

At is used for events, addresses or destinations.

We saw her sing *at* the opera.

They had dinner *at* Dave and Pauline's house.

I usually get off the train *at* North Melbourne.

PREPOSITION PHRASES

> A simple preposition phrase: *aside from, away from, in front of, in place of, on top of, out of, up to.*

Jade sat *in front of* the television.

> A preposition plus a noun phrase: *beside the river, between the flags, under the bridge.*

They had a picnic *beside the river.*

VERBS

> A verb is a word that is used to express action, mood, occurrence or state.

USE OF VERBS

➤ Verbs are used to say something about a person or thing.
➤ Verbs are used to make a statement, ask a question, give a command, make an exclamation or show ownership.
➤ Verbs are used in tenses – present, past, future and conditional.
➤ Verbs must agree with the subject in person and number.

He is a boy.

They are boys.

TYPES OF VERBS

The two main types are: ordinary (or principal) verbs and auxiliary verbs.

1. ORDINARY VERBS

a **Regular verbs** are verbs that have *-ed* or *-d* added to them for the past tense and the passive/past participle.

Play, played, played; love, loved, loved

b **Irregular verbs** do not have a regular pattern.

Some verbs do not change, regardless of the tense.

put, put, put; hit, hit, hit

Some verbs change their word pattern completely.

do, did, done; go, went, gone; eat, ate, eaten

See the list of irregular verbs on pages 73-76.

c **Transitive verbs** are verbs that take a direct object.

The man *killed a snake*.

Transitive verbs have two forms – active and passive. Active and passive verb forms show the relationship of the subject to the action.

› Active: the subject performs the action.

The boy *hit* the ball.

› Passive: the subject receives the action, or the agent of the action is unknown or not important.

The ball was hit by the boy. (The object becomes the subject)

See the section on passive verb forms (pages 69-71) for more information.

Direct and indirect objects:

Some verbs may have two objects.

› Indirect object: the person or animal named.
› Direct object: the thing named.

Lauren handed *me a book*. (*me* is the indirect object; *a book* is the direct object)

We made *all the girls a gift*. (*all the girls* is the indirect object; *a gift* is the direct object)

The sentences can be rearranged:

Lauren handed *a book to me*. (*a book* is still the direct object; *me* is still the indirect object, with *to*.)

We made *a gift for all the girls*. (*a gift* is still the direct object; *all the girls* is still the indirect object, with *for*.)

d **Intransitive verbs** are verbs that do not take a direct object and are not normally used in the passive verb form.

Birds *fly*.

Babies *cry*.

Fish *swim*.

› However, intransitive verbs often have a complement:

A preposition phrase:	Birds *fly* in the air.
An adverb:	Babies *cry* pitifully.
An adverb:	Fish *swim* quickly.

A *preposition phrase* or an *adverb* can be called an *adverbial*.

Note: Many verbs can be Transitive and Intransitive:

Jade *plays* the trumpet. (transitive)

Jade *plays* in the band. (intransitive)

2. AUXILIARY VERBS

There are two types of auxiliary verbs:

a **Plain auxiliary verbs** are used to form tenses: *be, do, have, will*

Present simple:	*Do* you *like* coffee? (do)
Present continuous:	I *am playing* soccer. (be)
Present perfect:	He *has gone* to the beach. (have)
Present perfect continuous:	I *have been watching* TV. (have, be)
Past simple:	He *didn't read* the book. (do)
Past continuous:	They *were driving* all night. (be)
Past perfect:	We *had joined* the club. (have)
Past perfect continuous:	You *had been eating* your dinner. (have, be)
Future simple:	I *will go* next week. (will)
Future continuous:	She *will be working* next year. (will, be)
Future perfect:	We *will have sold* our car by then. (will, have)
Future perfect continuous:	They *will have been driving* for ten hours. (will, have, be)

b **Modal auxiliary verbs (modals)** help show the meaning or mood of ordinary verbs. They have no infinitives: *can, could, may, might, must, will, would, shall, should, ought to, used to*. They are used with infinitives without *to*: *can have* (not *can to have*).

Requests:	*Can* I have an ice-cream please?
Possibility:	We *might* walk to the beach.
Permission:	You *may* go to the movies. (giving permission)
Permission:	*May* I have a drink, please? (asking for permission)
Ability:	Mark *can* drive a car.
Opportunity:	We *can* go to the park.
Obligation:	You *should* see the doctor.
Deduction:	It *could* be done.
Necessity:	You *must* go to the hospital immediately.
Offers:	*Would* you like a ticket?
Predictions:	It *might* rain tomorrow.
Decisions:	I *will* go to the movies with you.
Suggestions:	We *ought to* have a holiday.
Discontinued action:	I *used to* be able to ride a bike.

Note: *Will* functions as a plain auxiliary verb to indicate tense and as a modal verb to indicate intention.

More information about auxiliary verbs:

- Questions:

    Do you like the new car?

    Could we borrow your car please?

- Negatives:

    You *must not* go! (not goes after the auxiliary verb)

- *Be*, *have*, *used* and *ought* are followed by the infinitive with to.

    He *is to go* to England.

    I *have to read* this book.

    We *used to live* in a big house.

    They *ought to be* here to see this.

- *Do, can, may, must, will* and *shall* are followed by the infinitive without to.

    He *doesn't read* yet.

    Rosie *can swim*.

    You *may go*.

    Jan *must see* him.

    Bob *will help* you.

    We *shall meet* at the beach.

- Auxiliary verbs are usually contracted in conversation.

Be	*I'm* going home. (I am going home.)
Have	*We've* met them. (We have met them.)
Will	*She'll* come with me. (She will come with me.)

    Had and *would* have the same contraction.

    He'd gone to work. (He had gone to work.)

    He'd work with them. (He would work with them.)

    Is and *has* have the same contraction.

    He's going to fly that plane. (He is going to fly that plane.)

    He's gone to golf. (He has gone to golf.)

For more information and examples see Modal (auxiliary) verbs on pages 62-68.

MOODS OF VERBS

Moods of verbs show the frame of mind of the performer. There are four moods of verbs: three finite and one infinitive.

Finite moods

1 **INDICATIVE MOOD** is used to show fact. These verbs are either active or passive.

   He *stopped* the fight. (active)

   The fight *was stopped* by him. (passive)

2 **SUBJUNCTIVE MOOD** is used to express a doubt, a wish or a supposition – something that is not a fact. *If, unless, may* and *might* usually show that there is some doubt.

   He *might stop* the fight.

   The subjunctive mood is often *subjoined* to another clause and the form of the verb changes in many cases: *am/is* becomes *be*, *was* becomes *were*, and *has* becomes *have*.

   Be that as it may . . .

   If I *were* you . . .

   If I *were* a rich man . . .

   If you want the best team, let it *have* the best players.

3 **IMPERATIVE MOOD** is used to express a command. It is used in the present tense and in the second person (you): (*You, stop*!)

   Stop the fight!

Infinitive moods

4 **INFINITIVE MOOD** is used to show some action or state without reference to the doer of the action, the number, or the tense of the verb.

   He wanted *to stop* the fight.

THE INFINITIVE

English verbs are normally known by their infinitives – for example *to walk, to be, to sing, to pray, to have, to speak, to do*. The infinitive names the verb without referring to the doer of the action, the number, or the tense of the verb.

   If we look at the following sentence, it makes it clearer.

   Laurie and Maree want *to buy* a new house.

   to buy is the infinitive; *want* is the action verb.

Infinitives can be used as other parts of speech – nouns, adjectives or adverbs.

- The infinitive used as a noun:

  To forgive is very important. (the subject)

- The infinitive used as an adjective:

  They had many rules *to learn*. (describing rules)

- The infinitive used as an adverb:

  The children came inside *to read*. (modifying *came*)

The preposition *to* is not a necessary part of the infinitive.

- The infinitive with *to*:

  It's wonderful *to be* here.

  Are we allowed *to park* over there?

  John decided *to leave* early.

- The infinitive without *to*:

  They heard her *sing*.

  He really made me *cry*.

  We all watched the children *play*.

- An example of both – the infinitive with *to* and the infinitive without *to*:

  Laurie and Maree want *to go* and *buy* a new house.

The infinitive mentioned above is sometimes called the **present infinitive**. If the present form leaves a question, we can sometimes use the **perfect infinitive**.

We hoped *to see* their new house. (does not say if we saw the house)

We hoped *to have seen* their new house. (shows that we did not see the house)

Split infinitives occur when another word is placed between *to* and the verb. These are used mainly for dramatic effect.

To boldly go into the unknown.

Note: Infinitives are sometimes called verbals. A verbal is a verb form, but is used as another part of speech. There are 3 types of verbals: gerunds, infinitives and participles.

Dancing and *swimming* are Deanne's favourite pastimes. (gerunds)

James and Deanne decided *to rent* another house. (infinitive)

Smiling, Isabel welcomed the guests. (present participle)

Jenson was *tired*. (past participle)

VERB PHRASES

There are two types of verb phrases (see also pages 104-106).

1 **VERB PHRASES**: *is working, will take, can give, should have been*

   Stuart *is working* in a great job.

2 **PHRASAL VERBS** contain a verb plus an adverb: *take out, go away, turn around*

   Stuart *turned around* and saw Alison.

   Phrasal verbs can also contain a verb plus a preposition: *keep away from, come in from*

   Alison *came in from* the garden.

VERB TENSES

Verbs are used in tenses – present, past, future and conditional. Transitive verbs have two forms – active and passive. The following is a list of all the active verb tenses.

Present simple:	we *walk*
Present continuous:	we *are walking*
Present perfect:	we *have walked*
Present perfect continuous:	we *have been walking*
Past simple:	we *walked*
Past continuous:	we *were walking*
Past perfect:	we *had walked*
Past perfect continuous:	we *had been walking*
Future simple:	we *will walk*
Future continuous:	we *will be walking*
Future perfect:	we *will have walked*
Future perfect continuous:	we *will have been walking*
Present conditional:	we *would walk*
Present conditional continuous:	we *would be walking*
Perfect conditional:	we *would have walked*
Perfect conditional continuous:	we *would have been walking*

These verb tenses are further explained on the following pages.

The conditional tenses are generally taught in terms of function. See Conditionals on pages 59-61.

   Note: Look at the following table of main active verb tenses and you will see all the aspects of present, past and future verb tenses. You need to look at the table each time you write anything – an essay or a report, for example – to make sure that you use *all four aspects* of each tense. This will help you produce a really good piece of writing.

TABLE 2.2 The main active verb tenses

Present simple	Present continuous	Present perfect	Present perfect continuous
We *play* soccer every Saturday.	I *am playing* soccer with John. (I'm)	They *have played* soccer. (They've)	We *have been playing* soccer. (We've)
We *do not play* soccer in summer. (don't)	He *is not playing* soccer now. (isn't)	He *has not played* soccer. (hasn't)	They *have not been playing* soccer today. (haven't)
Do you *play* soccer?	*Are* you *playing* soccer?	*Have* you *played* soccer?	*Has* he *been playing* soccer today?
Past simple	**Past continuous**	**Past perfect**	**Past perfect continuous**
He *watched* the game yesterday.	He *was watching* the game yesterday.	He *had watched* the game all night (He'd)	He *had been watching* the game that day (He'd)
We *did not watch* the game. (didn't)	She *was not watching* the game last week. (wasn't)	They *had not watched* the game. (hadn't)	We *had not been watching* the game that day. (hadn't)
Did they *watch* the game?	*Were* they *watching* the game today?	*Had* he *watched* the game?	*Had* they *been watching* the game?
Future simple	**Future continuous**	**Future perfect**	**Future perfect continuous**
He *will work* tomorrow. (He'll)	I *will be working* then. (I'll)	She *will have worked* by then. (She'll)	We *will have been working* for 10 years by then. (We'll)
They *will not work*. (won't)	He *will not be working* then. (won't)	We *will not have worked* by then. (won't)	I *will not have been working* by then. (won't)
Will you *work* tomorrow?	*Will* you *be working* tomorrow?	*Will* you *have worked* by then?	*Will* he *have been working* by then?

Note: *I'm, I'll, we'll, we've, he'll, she'll, he'd, they've, didn't, wasn't, hadn't, hasn't, won't, don't* and *isn't* are **contractions**. See Chapter 3, pages 114-116 for more information.

VERB TENSES: PRESENT

PRESENT SIMPLE

➤ The present simple is used for repeated actions.

I *eat* breakfast every morning.

➤ The present simple is used for a permanent state.

I *am* a woman.

The earth *is* round.

➤ The present simple has the same form as the infinitive without *to*: for example, *love* and *go*.

I *love* a good movie.

However, with *he, she* or *it*, the verb has an 's' on the end (see note below).

He *loves* a good movie.

➤ The present simple is often used to express the future.

Dongli *goes* to China in June.

➤ The verb *to do* is used for questions and negatives, and the active verb uses the infinitive without *to*: for example, *go* and *want*:

Do and *Don't* for *I*, *you*, *we*, *they*.

Do you *go* tomorrow?

No, I *don't go* tomorrow.

Does and *Doesn't* for *he*, *she*, *it*.

Does she *want* an icecream?

No, she *doesn't want* an icecream.

Note: Most verbs have the same pattern – for *he*, *she* and *it* an 's' is put at the end of the verb.

Work	I, you, we, they	use *work*	I work, you work, we work, they work.
	he, she, it	use *works*	he works, she works, it works.
Read	I, you, we, they	use *read*	I read, you read, we read, they read.
	he, she, it	use *reads*	he reads, she reads, it reads.

There are some spelling differences:

Teach	I, you, we, they	use *teach*	I teach, you teach, we teach, they teach.
	he, she, it	use *teaches*	he teaches, she teaches, it teaches.
Fly	I, you, we, they	use *fly*	I fly, you fly, we fly, they fly.
	he, she, it	use *flies*	he flies, she flies, it flies.

> However, some verbs are different.

Be: I am; you are, we are, they are; he is, she is, it is.
Do: I do, you do, we do, they do; he does, she does, it does.
Have: I have, you have, we have, they have; he has, she has, it has.
Go: I go, you go, we go, they go; he goes, she goes, it goes.

Note: Use a dictionary if you are not sure how to spell a word.

Here is an example of some basic writing using present simple tense:

Everybody *loves* a holiday. In fact, everybody *needs* a holiday now and then. Some people *drive* to their holiday destination; some *catch* a bus or a train; and some *fly*.

When we *go* on holidays we usually *visit* family or friends. Many of our family members and friends *live* near a beach.

We *travel* by car or by plane. We *like* summer holidays best because we *enjoy* the beach. We *swim* each day in the surf and we *walk* along the water's edge in the evening.

We often *drive* to Melbourne or Sydney and we *fly* to Perth and *stay* with members of our family. We *don't catch* buses or trains very often. We *love* those cities and we *do* all sorts of interesting things in each of those cities. We *go* to wonderful restaurants in Melbourne; we *eat* fish and chips at the beaches in Sydney; and we *have* picnics in the parks in Perth.

If we *travel* overseas for a holiday we *become* tourists and we *enjoy* meeting people and learning about their country.

Do we *love* holidays? Absolutely!

PRESENT CONTINUOUS

- The present continuous is used for something happening now.

    He*'s eating* breakfast in the kitchen right now.

- The present continuous is used for an action happening about this time but not necessarily at the moment of speaking.

    I*'m reading* a book by my favourite author.

- The present continuous uses the present tense of the verb *to be* (am, is, are) plus the present participle (a verb with *-ing* on the end).

    I *am eating* an apple.

    She *is watching* television.

    We *are driving* in the car.

- The present continuous is used for a definite decision or arrangement in the near future.

    We *are going* to the beach tomorrow.

- The verb *to be* (am, is, are) plus the present participle (a verb with *-ing* on the end) is used for questions and negatives.

    Are you *cooking* dinner?

    No, I *am* (I'm) *not cooking* at the moment.

Here are some examples of present continuous tense:

   Deanne *is making* lunch for the children.

   James *is mowing* the lawn.

   Isabel and Jenson *are watching* a movie about animals.

   Isabel asks: 'Am I *going* to see some lions at the zoo tomorrow?'

   'No, *we're not going* to the zoo tomorrow.' replied Deanne.

   Isabel asks, 'When *are we going* to the zoo please?'

PRESENT PERFECT

- The present perfect is used to talk about the present and the past. There is a present result of a past action. Something was done in the past that still has a connection with the present.

    I *have bought* this new jacket. Isn't it great? (I still have it.)

    He *has lived* in Melbourne for 12 years. (He still lives in Melbourne.)

- The present perfect uses the present tense of the verb *to have* (have/has) plus a verb with a past participle. This means that you put *-ed* (walked) or *-d* (loved) at the end of regular verbs.

    For irregular verbs look at the list of irregular verbs on pages 73-76 and use the verbs in the columns headed 'Passive/past participle'.

    He *has lived* in Melbourne for 12 years. (regular verb)

    I *have bought* this new jacket. Isn't it great? (irregular verb)

    Note: With *he*, *she* or *it*, *have* becomes *has*.

    He *has washed* the clothes.

- The present perfect uses the verb *to have* (have/has) plus a verb with a past participle for questions and negatives.

    Have they *eaten*?

    She *hasn't looked* for a new car yet.

- The present perfect is usually contracted (shortened): *I have* becomes *I've* and *he has* becomes *he's*.

- The present perfect is often used with *gone to* and *been to*.

    Eun Joo *has gone* to Sydney. (She is there now.)

    Eun Joo *has been* to Perth. (The visit is over.)

- The present perfect is also often used with words such as *just, already, yet, today*, etc.

    I *have* just *eaten* lunch. (I'm still very full.)

    I *have* already *posted* the letter. (It's on its way.)

    Has it *stopped* raining yet? (It was raining a few minutes ago.)

    I've already *drunk* four cups of coffee today. (I can't take any more.)

- The present perfect is mainly used in conversations, letters, newspapers and television and radio reports.

Here are some examples of present perfect tense:

Fernando is looking for his car keys. He*'s lost* them.

He*'s bought* a new car. It's green.

He is happy because he *has started* a new job.

His friends *have gone* to the city.

He*'s visited* them three times this year.

Here are some questions using present perfect tense:

Have you ever *ridden* a horse?

Has she *moved* into her new house yet?

Maisy, *have* you *seen* Lauren today?

Have Rosie and Isabel *gone* to the park?

Has Tim *arrived* home yet?

Here is a dialogue using present perfect tense:

Bill: *Have* you *travelled* a lot, Bev?

Bev: Yes, I*'ve been* to lots of places.

Bill: Really? *Have* you ever *travelled* to Indonesia?

Bev: Yes, I*'ve been* to Indonesia twice.

Bill: What about India?

Bev: No, I *haven't been* to India.

Here is a dialogue using *gone to* and *been to* in the present perfect tense:

Demetrio: Where is Bartolomea?

Giovanni: She *has gone to* the shops with Bev.

Demetrio: I *have* just *been to* the shops with Andrea. I didn't see them.

Giovanni: Did you see Guglielmo there?

Demetrio: No, he *has gone to* the movies with his friends.

Giovanni: Oh, I wonder if he *has been to* the new theatre in the city.

Note: *gone to* – the person went and is still there; *been to* – the person went and is now back.

PRESENT PERFECT CONTINUOUS

➤ The present perfect continuous is used for an action over a period of time up to now.

We *have been driving* for six hours.

➤ The present perfect continuous is made up of the present tense of the verb *to have* (have/has) plus the past participle of the verb *to be* (been) plus the present participle (a verb with *-ing* on the end).

We *have been driving* for six hours.

Have becomes *has* when used with *he*, *she* and *it*.

She *has been working* for two hours.

➤ The present perfect continuous is usually contracted (shortened).

We*'ve been driving* for six hours.

She*'s been working* for two hours.

➤ For both questions and negatives the present perfect continuous uses *have* (have/has) plus *been* plus the present participle (a verb with *-ing* on the end).

Has Lauren *been playing* netball today?

No, Lauren *hasn't been playing* netball today.

Here are some examples of present perfect continuous tense:

I *have been washing* the clothes all day.

Jae Sung *has been cutting* the lawn and is exhausted.

Annie is very tired. She *has been typing* this book all day.

Isabel *has been sleeping* all day. She must be tired.

Let's go and visit Vasco and Acacio. They *have been working* this morning.

Leanne and Mark *have been living* in their house for ten years.

Has Raquel *been reading* that new book?

No, Raquel *hasn't been reading* that book. Lucia *has been reading* it.

Have the children *been swimming* all morning?

No, they *haven't been swimming* for that long.

VERB TENSES: PAST

PAST SIMPLE

➤ The past simple is used for something done in the past, which is finished.

We *lived* in Sydney for six years. (We don't live there now.)

➤ The regular verbs in past simple tense end in *-d* or *-ed*: *dance(d)*, *call(ed)*.

Sara *danced* beautifully and the audience *called* for an encore. (The performance is over)

➤ For the irregular verbs in past simple tense, see the list of irregular verbs on pages 73-76 and look at the past tense column.

He *felt* really sick when he *broke* his nose. (His nose is fine now.)

➤ The verb *to do* is used in its past tense form (did) for questions and negatives. *Did* is also used for all persons: *I, you, she, he, it, we, they*.

Did you *go* to the movies yesterday?

No, I *didn't like* any of the movies that were showing.

➤ For both questions and negatives, *to do* is in its past tense form (did), but the active verb uses the infinitive without *to*, for example *go* and *like*.

Did he *go* to the beach yesterday? RIGHT

Did he *went* to the beach yesterday? WRONG

No, he *didn't like* the weather. RIGHT

No, he *didn't liked* the weather. WRONG

Here are some examples using past simple tense:

It *was* hot, so I *took* off my coat. (*be* and *take*)

The movie *was* awful. We *didn't enjoy* it very much. (*be* and *enjoy*)

Wendy *was* busy, so I *didn't ring* her. (*be* and *ring*)

I *missed* you. Where *did* you *go*? (*miss* and *go*)

I *was* late for work because I *slept* in. (*be* and *sleep*)

I *sold* my car yesterday. (*sell*)

I *ate* a huge breakfast this morning. (*eat*)

He *didn't come* home last night. (*come*)

Did you *enjoy* the show? (*enjoy*)

PAST CONTINUOUS

- The past continuous is used for something that was happening in the past.

    They *were watching* television when their friends arrived.

- The past continuous uses the past tense of the verb *to be* (was/were) plus the present participle (a verb with *-ing* on the end).

    As he *was mowing* the lawn, the lawn mower ran out of fuel.

    Our friends arrived while we *were eating* lunch.

- The past continuous is used to explain the background to a situation that happened in the past.

    The rain *was falling*, so I ran for the bus and tripped over.

    The children *were waiting* and then suddenly Santa Claus arrived.

- The past continuous and the past simple combine to explain what was happening when something occurred.

    I went to sleep and got sunburnt while I *was lying* on the beach.

    (The past simple verbs in the sentence are *went* and *got*.)

- The verb *to be* is used in the past tense (was/were) plus the present participle (a verb with *-ing* on the end) for questions and negatives.

    Was he *painting* that room last week?

    Were they *working* in 1992?

    We *weren't playing* soccer last year.

Here are some examples of past continuous tense:

   I broke the vase. I *was taking* it into the lounge room and I tripped over the dog. (take)

   The dog *was walking* past the doorway as I *was going* into the room and I tripped over it. (walk and go)

   I *wasn't looking* where I *was walking*. (look and walk)

Here are some more examples of past continuous tense:

Richard:	*Was* Tim *playing* soccer today?
Sue:	No, he *was doing* Tae Kwon Do.
Richard:	Lauren *was swimming* today. I thought she *was playing* soccer.
Sue:	No, Tim, Lauren and Rosie *were playing* soccer last year.
Richard:	Rosie told me she *wasn't going* to soccer this year.
Sue:	That's right, she *was playing* hockey last night.

PAST PERFECT

- The past perfect is used to explain an action before a past time.

   We missed the train because we *had gone* to sleep.

- The past perfect uses the past tense of the verb *to have* (had) plus a verb with a past participle.

   To make a past participle means that you put *-ed* (walk*ed*) or *-d* (move*d*) at the end of a regular verb. For irregular verbs look at the list of irregular verbs on pages 73-76 and use the words in the column headed 'Passive/past participle'.

   The men went into the clubhouse after they *had played* golf.

   We missed the train because we *had gon*e to sleep.

- The past perfect uses the past tense of the verb *to have* (had) for all persons.

   James gave Deanne the book because he *had read* it.

   We went to the concert because *we'd bought* some tickets.

- For both questions and negatives the past perfect uses *had* plus a verb using the past participle.

   Had you *read* that book before James gave it to Deanne?

   No, I *hadn't finished* the book, but he didn't know that.

- Note the difference:

   When we arrived the children *ate* their dinner. (when we arrived: past simple)

   When we arrived, the children *had eaten* their dinner. (before we arrived: past perfect)

- The past perfect is often used with *before*, *until* and *just*.

   I *had hit* the tree *before* I realised it was there.

   She didn't go to bed *until* she *had cleaned* her teeth.

   They *had just assassinated* Julius Caesar when Antony arrived.

Here are some examples of past perfect tense:

Rainer gave the book to his friend because he *had read* it.

Palma looked after Michael as Nadine *had driven* to the shops.

Yea Kyung told us about the movie that she *had seen* last week.

Mi Ran spoke about the time she *had travelled* overseas.

When I arrived, Ezra *had* just *left*.

Caroline *had arrived* in Switzerland when she rang us.

Olga *had lived* near us before she went to the city.

Had they *been* to Vietnam when they met up with Tuk in Thailand?

Juan didn't have a rest even though he *had worked* all day.

Jasper told Jamie that he *had gone* to England for a holiday.

I *hadn't finished* the job when the computer crashed

Note: The past perfect tense is used to explain an action before a past time. The previous action in these sentences is underlined.

Ten people *had eaten* fish. They all got sick. (They ate the fish first.)

The postman gave me my letters. I*'d seen* him coming.

He *had played* the piano very well. We all stood and clapped.

I gave the book to my friend. I *had read* it.

She was delighted because she *hadn't read* it.

I *had washed* the dishes. I put them away.

I drove off in my car. I *had looked* both ways.

The men *had played* golf. They went into the clubhouse.

We didn't stop until we*'d finished* the job.

We didn't have a car last week. We*'d sold* our old one.

Had Bill *finished* work when Lesley rang?

No, but Lesley *had done* the shopping and needed his help.

Bill went to the shops where Lesley and Lisa *had gone*.

PAST PERFECT CONTINUOUS

➤ The past perfect continuous is used for an action that was happening in the past and finished in the past.

She *had been waiting* for three days before the parcel arrived.

We *had been living* on the coast before we moved to our new house.

➤ The past perfect continuous is made up of the past tense of the verb *to have* (had) plus the past participle of the verb *to be* (been) plus the present participle (a verb with *-ing* on the end).

We *had been driving* for hours when we ran out of petrol.

➤ For both questions and negatives the past perfect continuous uses *had* plus *been* plus the present participle (a verb with *-ing* on the end).

Had you been running when you fell over?

No, I *hadn't been running*, I just fell over the dog.

Here are some examples of past perfect continuous tense:

There was water in the cupboard because the tap *had been leaking*. (*leak*)

They were exhausted because they *had been walking* all day. (*walk*)

The baby was happy because she *had been sleeping*. (*sleep*)

We always visited Grandma after she *had been making* toffee. (*make*)

We left our home after we *had been living* there for years. (*live*)

Had they *been sleeping* when the siren rang? (*sleep*)

No they *hadn't been sleeping* before it rang. (*sleep*)

Here are some more examples of past perfect continuous:

Barbara *had been cooking* all day and was tired.

Yuki was happy to be home as she *had been flying* for hours.

Tomoko *had been sleeping* when Yuki rang from New York.

Had Tomoko *been working* when Yuki rang before?

Caroline arrived in Zurich after she *had been travelling* all night.

Ueli and Marianne *hadn't been waiting* very long when their friends arrived.

Margaret was really tired. She *had been gardening* all day.

Gillian *had been reading* the newspaper when her visitors arrived.

David took some photos after Wendy *had been painting*.

VERB TENSES: FUTURE

➤ The main tenses use *will* (or *shall*).

  I *will bake* a cake tomorrow. (*I'll*) (future simple)

  I *will be baking* tomorrow. (*I'll*) (future continuous)

  I *will have baked* tomorrow. (future perfect)

  I *will have been baking* tomorrow. (future perfect continuous)

➤ *Will* and *shall* are auxiliary verbs.

➤ *Shall* is only used in the first person in the future: I and we.

  I *shall be* in Japan by the time you receive this letter. (or I *will be*)

Future simple *will* (or *shall*) plus the infinitive without *to*

  I *will/shall go* to the shops tomorrow. (statement)

  Will/shall I *work* tomorrow? (question)

  I *will/shall not work* tomorrow. (negative: *will not* can be *won't*)

  Note: The infinitive names the verb without referring to the doer, the number, or the tense, for example *to be, to bake*, etc.

  He wanted *to go* to the movies. (the infinitive with *to*)

  He will *go* to the movies. (the infinitive without *to*)

Future continuous *will* (or *shall*) plus *be* plus the present participle (a verb with -ing on the end)

  I *will be swimming* tomorrow. (statement)

  Will I *be swimming* tomorrow? (question)

  I *won't be swimming* tomorrow. (negative) (*won't = will not*)

Future perfect *will* (or *shall*) plus *have* plus a verb using the past participle

  In December, we *will have lived* in this house for 12 years. (statement)

  Will we *have lived* here that long? (question)

  We *won't have lived* here that long, surely. (negative)

Future perfect continuous *will* (or *shall*) plus *have* plus *been* plus the present participle (a verb with -ing on the end)

  We *shall have been driving* for eight hours. (statement)

  Will we *have been driving* for eight hours? (question)

  We *won't have been driving* for that long. (negative)

Other ways of expressing the future

- Present simple tense:

    Aili *goes* to Russia next week. (meaning she will go)

    I *leave* for Sydney tonight. (meaning I will go)

- Present continuous tense:

    Marie *is flying* to China this year. (meaning she will go)

    Is she *flying* to Russia? (question)

    No, she*'s not flying* to Russia. (negative)

    Note: The use of the present continuous tense for the future is just as common as the use of *will* and *shall*.

- The *be going* form for the future tense:

    I'm going to get a job.

    She*'s not going* to be there.

Here are some examples of the future tense:

Jan *will exhibit* her paintings next Sunday.

She *won't sell* that beautiful miniature.

Will Jan *have been painting* for long?

Yes, she*'ll have been painting* for months.

Gillian and Mike *are going* overseas soon.

Will Bonnie *stay* at home?

No, she *won't remain* at home.

They *are not going* to be home for weeks.

Claudia *moves* to her new home in August.

We*'ll miss* Claudia when she leaves.

Is Lucie *coming* to art classes again?

She *won't have been painting* for a long time.

Juanita *will be visiting* us soon.

Will Tara *be taking* Rosemary to the exhibition?

They *won't be going* this week.

Marilyn *will have gone* on holidays by May.

Will she *have travelled* with the family?

She *won't have gone* by herself.

CONDITIONALS

Conditional sentences are used to discuss things that can, or could, only occur under certain conditions.

Conditional sentences have two parts: the *if* clause and the main clause.

If it is sunny (*if* clause) we will go to the beach (main clause).

There are 4 main types of Conditional sentences.

Zero Conditional

These sentences express a simple consequence that is a fact. We can use *if, when,* or *whenever* and both clauses are usually in the Present Simple tense:

If water *freezes* it *turns* to ice.

When you *don't eat* you *lose* weight.

Whenever you *mix* two primary colours, you *get* a secondary colour.

First Conditional

These sentences express a real possibility and contain a different pair of tenses.

If I win the cup, I will give it to my father.

If I *win* the cup	(the *if* clause is using Present Simple tense)
I *will give* it to my father.	(the main clause is using Future Simple tense)

Second Conditional

These sentences express something that is not a real possibility and contain a different pair of tenses.

If I won the cup, I would give it to my father.

If I *won* the cup	(the *if* clause is using Past Simple tense)
I *would give* it to my father.	(the main clause is using Present Conditional tense)

Third Conditional

These sentences express something that cannot be a possibility because the action in the *if* clause didn't happen and contain a different pair of tenses.

If I had won the cup, I would have given it to my father.

If I *had won* the cup	(the if clause is using Past Perfect tense)
I *would have given* it to my father.	(the main clause is using Perfect Conditional tense)

TABLE 2.3 Conditionals

Conditional	Likelihood of event	Example	Tense
Zero	The result is *always* true.	If you *heat* ice, it *melts*.	Present simple
First	*May* or *may not* happen	If it *is* sunny tomorrow,	Present simple
		we *will go* to the beach.	Future simple
Second	*Unlikely* to happen	If I *won* the lottery,	Past simple
		I *would take* my family on a holiday.	Present conditional
Third	*Impossible*	If I *had won* the lottery,	Past perfect
		I *would have taken* my family on a holiday.	Perfect conditional

Conditional tenses

    Present conditional: We *would walk*. (affirmative)

                                                  Would we *walk*? (question)

                                                  We *wouldn't walk*. (negative)

    Present conditional continuous: We *would be walking*. (affirmative)

                                                  Would we *be walking*? (question)

                                                  We *wouldn't be walking*. (negative)

    Perfect conditional: We *would have walked*. (affirmative)

                                                  Would we *have walked*? (question)

                                                  We *wouldn't have walked*. (negative)

    Perfect conditional continuous: We *would have been walking*. (affirmative)

                                                  Would we *have been walking*? (question)

                                                  We *wouldn't have been walking*. (negative)

Note: With *I* and *we*, *would* or *should* can be used.

If you had asked me, I *should/would* have gone.

We *should/would* have asked you if we thought you had wanted to go.

> **The present conditional** uses *would* plus the infinitive (without *to*).

  Songkan *would go* to China if she had a ticket.

> **The present conditional** is used as a past equivalent of the future tense.

  Sailosi *will go* to China if he is given a ticket. (future tense)

  Sailosi *would go* to China, if he had a ticket. (present conditional)

> **The present conditional continuous** uses *would* plus *be* plus the present participle (a verb with *-ing* on the end).

  Caleb *would be working*, if he hadn't sustained those injuries.

> **The perfect conditional** uses *would* plus *have* plus a verb with a past participle.

  Benji *would have played* if there had been more time.

> **The perfect conditional** is also used as a past equivalent of the future tense.

  Isabel and Jenson *will have eaten* if Deanne comes home late. (future tense)

  Isabel and Jenson *would have eaten* if Deanne had come home late. (perfect conditional)

Here are more examples of Conditional Sentences

If I eat too much I get fat.	(Zero Conditional)
What happens if/when you eat too much?	(Zero Conditional)
If/whenever you don't eat you get hungry.	(Zero Conditional)
If Soomin sends the letter today it will arrive by Christmas.	(1st Conditional)
Will you come with me, if I pay the fare?	(1st Conditional)
He won't go to the beach, even if they ask him.	(1st Conditional)
If Soomin left, Joo Eun would pick her up from the airport.	(2nd Conditional)
Would you buy a second-hand car, if I gave you money?	(2nd Conditional)
I wouldn't buy a second-hand car, even if you paid me.	(2nd Conditional)
Fen would've gone, if she had bought a ticket.	(3rdConditional)
Would you have gone if she had bought a ticket?	(3rd Conditional)
We wouldn't have driven to the beach, if it had rained.	(3rd Conditional)

MODAL (AUXILIARY) VERBS

Modal auxiliary verbs (modals) help to show the meaning or mood of ordinary verbs. They have no infinitive: *can, could, may, might, must, will, would, shall, should, ought to, used to*. They are also used with infinitives without *to*: *can go* (not *can to go*).

TABLE 2.4 Table of Modal Verbs with negatives and contractions

Modal verb	Negative form	Contraction
can	cannot	can't
could	could not	couldn't
may	may not	-
might	might not	mightn't
must	must not	musn't
will	will not	won't
would	would not	wouldn't
shall	shall not	shan't
should	should not	shouldn't
ought to	ought not	oughtn't*
used to	didn't use to / used not*	-

* Note: *oughtn't* and *used not* are seldom used.

How to use *can*, *could*, *may*, *might* and *must*

Can

➤ Someone **has** the ability or opportunity to do something.

   I *can* type a letter. (ability)

   She *can* eat more than her sister. (ability)

   We *can* all swim very well. (ability)

   We *can* sit on the grass if it is dry. (opportunity)

   You *can* order steak at that restaurant. (opportunity)

   They *can* swim in that pool. (opportunity)

➤ Question:

   Can I drive well enough for my licence? (ability)

   Can I watch TV please, Mum? (opportunity)

- Negative:

    He *can't* drive a car yet. (ability)

    I *can't* go to the movies tonight. (opportunity)

Could

- Someone **had** the ability or opportunity to do something in the past.

    Wendy *could* run very fast when she was younger. (ability)

    I *could* eat chocolate, but I can't now. It gives me a headache. (ability)

    He *could* ski before he broke his leg. (ability)

    We *could* see Ron mending the pipe. (opportunity)

    I *could* have fish at that cafe last week. (opportunity)

    We *could* ski in that place last winter. (opportunity)

- Question:

    Could they fix the TV? (ability)

    Could you see the snow on the mountain? (opportunity)

- Negative:

    I *couldn't* understand him. (ability)

    John *couldn't* play golf in the rain. (opportunity)

Can, may and could - permission

- Asking permission: *can*, *could* and *may*

    Can I use your pen please? (casual)

    Could I use your pen please? (more polite)

    May I use your pen please? (very polite or formal)

    Can I grab some chips please? (very casual)

    Could I take your order, sir? (more polite)

    May I have another coffee please? (very polite)

    Can we go for a swim? (very casual)

    Could we have a ride in your boat, please? (more polite)

    May I see your tickets please, sir? (very polite)

- Giving permission: use *can* or *may* (but not *could*). *May* is formal.

    You *can* borrow my car. (casual)

    You *may* borrow my car. (very polite or formal)

You *can* have chips with your fish. (casual)

You *may* sit near the window. (polite)

You *can* swim in the pool. (casual)

You *may* have a ride in my boat. (polite)

> Refusing permission: use *can* or *may* (but not *could*). *May* is formal.

You *can't* borrow my car. (casual)

You *may not* borrow my car. (formal, but firm)

You *can't* smoke in this cafe. (casual)

You *may not* bring children to this restaurant. (polite, but firm)

You *can't* take children to that resort. (casual, but firm)

He *may not* smoke here. (polite, but firm)

> Talking about permission: use *can* for the present and future. Use *could* for the past.

I *can* borrow his book. (present)

I *can't* borrow his book tomorrow. (future)

I *could* borrow his book last week. (past)

May, might and could - possibility

> *May* and *might*: something is very possible – present and future.

There *may/might* be some hot soup in the kitchen. (present)

I *may/might* be late for work tomorrow. (future)

There *may* be coffee left in the pot. (present)

We *might* be able to see that movie next week. (future)

There *may* be some tickets available for that flight. (present)

There *might* be a few seats available later. (future)

> *Could*: something is possible – present and future.

There *could* be some hot soup in the kitchen. (present)

I *could* go to the movies tonight. (future)

There *could* be some oysters left, but I'm not sure. (present)

There *could* be some snow tomorrow. (future)

> *May not/might not*: something is almost impossible.

There *may not/might not* be any seats left. (mightn't)

I *may not/might not* have time to go.

You *may not/might* not be able to drive that car.

- *Could not*: something is impossible.

    I was sick, so I *couldn't* work.

    He *could not* go to the shops because they were closed.

May, might and must – an opportunity showing different degrees of urgency

    I am feeling sick; I *may* go to the doctor. (not very urgent)

    I am feeling very sick; I *might* go to the doctor. (somewhat urgent)

    I am feeling terribly sick; I *must* go to the doctor. (extremely urgent)

- *Must*: showing something is necessary

    You *must* smoke outside.

    You *must* swim between the flags.

Must and *can't* are used as opposites

- *Must* is used when we think something is true.

    Paul isn't at work today. He *must* be sick.

    Katie misplaced her keys. They *must* be in her car.

- *Can't* is used when we think something is not possible.

    It's only lunchtime. You *can't* be tired.

    Ana *can't* be lost. She had a map.

How to use *will*, *would*, *shall*, *should*, *ought to* and *used to*

Will – for predictions (future)

    Julie has worked all day. She *will* sleep well tonight.

    You *will* love that restaurant.

- Question:

    Do you think Julie *will* sleep well tonight?

    Will you order the fish for your dinner?

- Negative:

    Julie is very excited. She *won't* sleep tonight.

    You *won't* know if you like seafood, until you try it.

Would – for a prediction in the past or for a prediction of a possible event

Julie had worked all day. She knew she *would* sleep well. (past)

It *would* be nice to have some coffee later. (possible)

> Question:

Would you have liked that movie? (past)

Would you like to go to the movies? (possible)

> Negative:

No, I *wouldn't* have wanted to see that movie, thanks. (past)

She *wouldn't* want to miss out on that movie. (possible)

Will – for a decision or an offer

I *will* have a drink, please. (decision)

I *will* go to Singapore for my next holiday.

I'll give you a lift if you like. (offer)

I'll make you some coffee if you wait.

> Question:

Will you have a drink with me? (offer)

Will you come with me, Nate?

> Negative:

I *won't* have a drink, thank you. (decision)

I *won't* use the camera again.

Would – for a refusal in the negative

We tried to use the computer, but it *wouldn't* operate.

We tried to have some drinks, but they *wouldn't* serve us.

She wanted to use the camera, but it *wouldn't* work.

Shall – for offers or suggestions (only with *I* and *we*)

Shall I make a cup of tea? (offer)

Shall I drive you to the airport?

Shall we have a picnic? (suggestion)

Shall we go to the beach today?

Shall I ring that camping ground?

Should – for what is the right (or best) thing to do

You *should* go to the doctor.

We *should* get to the restaurant on time.

They *should* keep their baby out of the sun.

➤ Question:

Should I go to the doctor?

➤ Negative:

You *shouldn't* wait until you're too ill to go.

Ought to – for what is the right (or best) thing to do

You *ought to* stop working and have a rest.

Used to – for a discontinued action. Something that happened on a regular basis, or went on for some time in the past

We *used to* swim at that beach.

They *used to* live in Manchester.

Note: For questions and negatives we use *did*, and *used to* becomes *use to*.

➤ Question:

Did he use to live in the city?

➤ Negative:

He didn't use to live in the city.

Review of modal (auxiliary) verbs in a dialogue: *can, could, may, might, must, will, would, shall, should, ought to* and *used to*:

Dave:	Pauline, *would* you like to go camping with the family next week?
Pauline:	Yes, I'*d* love to. Where *shall* we go?
Dave:	We *could* go to the beach and we *can* camp there.
Pauline:	Good idea. *Can* we take surf boards?
Dave:	Yes, we *can*. I *used to* surf every day on holiday.
Pauline:	*Could* we take some bikes too?
Dave:	Yes, we *can* if I put the roof racks on the car. We *should* be able to take the kids' bikes too so they *can* ride them.
Pauline:	They'*ll* love it.
Dave:	We *must* get some camping gear before we go.
Pauline:	Yes, we *won't* be able to use our old gear.
Dave:	That's OK. Julie and Adrian *might* have some extra camping gear.
Pauline:	We'*ll* be fine. Remember we *could* borrow some last year.
Dave:	Yes, I *may* be able to get some from Wendy and Matt.
Pauline:	*Shall* we ring them straight away?
Dave:	Yes, we *ought to* give them some notice. Good idea!

PASSIVE VERB FORMS

➤ Passive verb forms (passive voice) change a sentence from the active to the passive. (Active = the subject doing the action. Passive = the subject receiving the action.)

That man *stole* my car. (active)

My car *was stolen* by that man. (passive)

Note: When changing a sentence from the active to the passive, the **object** becomes the **subject**.

➤ The passive verb form is mostly used in writing and when it is more interesting to stress the thing done than the doer of it – or when the doer is unknown.

The Dutch competitor *won* the championship. (active)

The championship *was won* by the Dutch competitor. (passive)

➤ The passive verb form uses the verb *to be* plus a passive/past participle. That means that you put *-d* or *-ed* at the ends of regular verbs, for example *moved, walked*. For irregular verbs, see the list on pages 73-76 and use the verbs in the columns headed 'Passive/past participle'.

Converting active to passive:

Present simple: We *keep* the children inside when it rains. (active)

The children *are kept* inside when it rains. (passive)

Present continuous: Are they *helping* the injured man? (active)

Is the injured man *being helped*? (passive)

Present perfect: We *haven't seen* kangaroos in this street. (active)

Kangaroos *haven't been seen* in this street. (passive)

Past simple: Hien *moved* the television. (active)

The television *was moved* by Hien. (passive)

Past continuous: They *were carrying* the injured man to the ambulance. (active)

The injured man *was being carried* to the ambulance. (passive)

Past perfect: They *had washed* the car when it rained. (active)

The car *had been washed* when it rained. (passive)

Future simple: Mark *will teach* those students. (active)

Those students *will be taught* by Mark. (passive)

Present conditional: Leanne *would do* that job. (active)

That job *would be done* by Leanne. (passive)

Perfect conditional: Isabel *would have eaten* that cake. (active)

That cake *would have been eaten* by Isabel. (passive)

Present infinitive: Aili *wants to plant* those trees in her garden. (active)

Those trees *are to be planted* in Aili's garden. (passive)

Perfect infinitive: We hoped *to have driven* him to the airport. (active)

He hoped *to have been driven* to the airport. (passive)

➤ Modal verbs in the passive verb form:

After *can, must, should, ought to*, etc, use *be* plus a passive/past participle:

John *can fly* that plane. (active)

That plane *can be flown* by John. (passive: *can be*)

You *must renew* your passport. (active)

Your passport *must be renewed*. (passive: *must be*)

They *should take* the dog to the vet. (active)

The dog *should be taken* to the vet. (passive: *should be*)

You *ought to open* the doors. (active)

The doors *ought to be opened*. (passive: *ought to be*)

➤ The passive verb form with and without *by*.

When we want to say who or what did the action we use *by*:

That masterpiece *was painted by* Jan.

When we want to say when or where something happens, we can use *in*, *to* or *at*:

That masterpiece *was painted in* 2008.

The masterpiece *will be taken to* the Exhibition.

The doors *will be opened* at 8.30am.

➤ The passive verb form is used especially in textbooks and reports. It is used to explain activities in science, industry and technology. It is used in news reports.

Minerals *are exported* to China.

Information *can be found* in those books or online.

Discussions *are being held* in New York today.

➤ The passive verb form sometimes uses the verb *to get* instead of the verb *to be* plus a passive/past participle. It is used mainly in casual English:

The man *cleans* her house. (active)

Her house *gets cleaned* by that man. (passive)

Who *broke* the window? (active)

How did the window *get broken*? (passive)

Here are some examples in the active and then passive verb forms:

They *cancelled* the flight yesterday. (active)
The flight *was cancelled* yesterday. (passive)

People *were using* that road every day. (active)
That road *was being used* every day, by some people. (passive)

I *have washed* the car. (active)
The car *has been washed*. (passive)

They *are going to sell* the house next week. (active)
Their house *is going to be sold* next week. (passive)

We *must register* the dog tomorrow. (active)
The dog *must be registered* tomorrow. (passive)

He *had taken* the prisoner to jail. (active)
The prisoner *had been taken* to jail by that man. (passive)

Deanne *will take* Jenson to the pool. (active)
Jenson *will be taken* to the pool by Deanne. (passive)

Mark *would paint* that scene. (active)
That scene *would be painted* by Mark. (passive)

Michael *is to do* the job in Helsinki. (active)
The job in Helsinki *is to be done* by Michael. (passive)

The children *make* sandcastles at the beach. (active)
Sandcastles *are made* at the beach. (passive)

James *will celebrate* his birthday in April. (active)
His birthday *will be celebrated* in April. (passive)

May *is drawing* some pictures. (active)
Those pictures *are being drawn* by May. (passive)

Jade *would have played* the trumpet solo. (active)
The trumpet solo *would have been played* by Jade. (passive)

IRREGULAR VERBS

Some active verbs do not have a regular pattern for their past and passive/past forms. Use the list on the following pages as a guide to those verbs that don't take -ed or -d for the past tense and passive/past participle.

For present simple tense

Some irregular verbs have different spelling patterns in the present simple tense.

➤ Most verbs have the same pattern: for *he*, *she* and *it* an 's' is put at the end of the verb.

| *Read* | I, you, we, they | use *read* | I read, you read, we read, they read. |
| | he, she, it | use *reads* | he reads, she reads, it reads. |

➤ There are some spelling differences:

| *Teach* | I, you, we, they | use *teach* | I teach, you teach, we teach, they teach. |
| | he, she, it | use *teaches* | he teaches, she teaches, it teaches. |

| *Fly* | I, you, we, they | use *fly* | I fly, you fly, we fly, they fly. |
| | he, she, it | use *flies* | he flies, she flies, it flies. |

➤ However, some verbs are different.

Be: I am; you are, we are, they are; he is, she is, it is.
Do: I do, you do, we do, they do; he does, she does, it does.
Have: I have, you have, we have, they have; he has, she has, it has.
Go: I go, you go, we go, they go; he goes, she goes, it goes.

For further information about present simple tense, see pages 46-47.

Use the list on the following pages as a guide to those verbs that do not take -ed or -d for the past tense or the passive/past participle.

➤ The verbs *to be*, *to have* and *to do* are explained in full following the list of irregular verbs.

TABLE 2.5 List of irregular verbs (square brackets indicate pronunciation)

Infinitive	Past tense	Passive/past participle	Infinitive	Past tense	Passive/past participle
A			burst	burst	burst
arise	arose	arisen	buy	bought	bought
awake	awoke	awoken	**C**		
B			cast	cast	cast
be	was/were	been	catch	caught	caught
bear	bore	borne	choose	chose	chosen
beat	beat	beaten	cling	clung	clung
become	became	become	come	came	come
befall	befell	befallen	cost	cost	cost
begin	began	begun	creep	crept	crept
behold	beheld	beheld	cut	cut	cut
bend	bent	bent	**D**		
bet	bet	bet	deal	dealt [delt]	dealt [delt]
beseech	besought	besought	dig	dug	dug
bid (order)	bade	bidden	dive	dived dove (US)	dived dived
bid (to offer)	bid	bid	do	did	done
bind	bound	bound	draw	drew	drawn
bite	bit	bitten	dream	dreamt [dremt] dreamed	dreamt [dremt] dreamed
bleed	bled	bled			
blow	blew	blown			
break	broke	broken			
breed	bred	bred	drink	drank	drunk
bring	brought	brought	drive	drove	driven
broadcast	broadcast	broadcast	dwell	dwelt dwelled	dwelt dwelled
build	built	built			
burn	burnt burned	burnt burned	**E**		
			eat	ate	eaten

Infinitive	Past tense	Passive/past participle	Infinitive	Past tense	Passive/past participle
F			hold	held	held
fall	fell	fallen	hurt	hurt	hurt
feed	fed	fed	**K**		
feel	felt	felt	keep	kept	kept
fight	fought	fought	kneel	knelt	knelt
find	found	found	know	knew	known
flee	fled	fled	**L**		
fling	flung	flung	lay	laid	laid
fly	flew	flown	lead	led	led
forbid	forbade	forbidden	lean	leant [lent] leaned	leant [lent] leaned
forget	forgot	forgotten			
forgive	forgave	forgiven	leap	leapt [lept] leaped	leapt [lept] leaped
forsake	forsook	forsaken			
foretell	foretold	foretold	learn	learnt learned	learnt learned
freeze	froze	frozen			
G			leave	left	left
get	got	got gotten(US)	lend	lent	lent
			let	let	let
give	gave	given	lie	lay	lain
go	went	gone	light	lit lighted	lit lighted
grind	ground	ground			
grow	grew	grown	lose	lost	lost
H			**M**		
hang	hung	hung	make	made	made
have	had	had	mean	meant	meant
hear	heard	heard	meet	met	met
hide	hid	hidden	mow	mowed	mown mowed
hit	hit	hit			

Infinitive	Past tense	Passive/past participle	Infinitive	Past tense	Passive/past participle
O			shear	shore / sheared	shorn / sheared
overtake	overtook	overtaken			
P			shed	shed	shed
pay	paid	paid	shine	shone	shone
prove	proved	proven / proved	shoe	shod / shoed	shod / shoed
put	put	put	shoot	shot	shot
R			show	showed	shown / showed
read [reed]	read [red]	read [red]			
rend	rent	rent	shrink	shrank / shrunk	shrunk / shrunk
rid	rid	rid			
ride	rode	ridden	shut	shut	shut
ring	rang	rung	sing	sang	sung
rise	rose	risen	sink	sank	sunk
run	ran	run	sit	sat	sat
S			slay	slew	slain
saw	sawed	sawn / sawed	sleep	slept	slept
			slide	slid	slid
say	said	said	sling	slung	slung
see	saw	seen	slink	slunk	slunk
seek	sought	sought	slit	slit	slit
sell	sold	sold	smell	smelt / smelled	smelt / smelled
send	sent	sent			
set	set	set	smite	smote	smitten
sew	sewed	sewn / sewed	sow	sowed	sown / sowed
shake	shook	shaken	speak	spoke	spoken

Infinitive	Past tense	Passive/past participle	Infinitive	Past tense	Passive/past participle
speed	sped speeded	sped speeded	swell	swelled	swollen swelled
spell	spelt spelled	spelt spelled	swim	swam	swum
			swing	swung	swung
spend	spent	spent	**T**		
spill	spilt spilled	spilt spilled	take	took	taken
			teach	taught	taught
spin	spun	spun	tear (rip)	tore	torn
spit	spat	spat	tell	told	told
split	split	split	think	thought	thought
spoil	spoilt spoiled	spoilt spoiled	throw	threw	thrown
			thrust	thrust	thrust
spread	spread	spread	tread	trod	trodden
spring	sprang	sprung	**U**		
stand	stood	stood	understand	understood	understood
steal	stole	stolen	undertake	undertook	undertaken
stick	stuck	stuck	**W**		
sting	stung	stung	wake	woke waked	woken waked
stink	stank stunk	stunk stunk			
			wear	wore	worn
stride	strode	stridden	weave	wove weaved	woven weaved
strike	struck	struck (stricken)			
			weep	wept	wept
string	strung	strung	win	won	won
strive	strove	striven	wind	wound	wound
swear	swore	sworn	wring	wrung	wrung
sweep	swept	swept	write	wrote	written

The verb *to be*

The verb *to be* is the most important verb in the English language. It is also a verb that is hard to recognise because it is made up of three (some argue four) different verbs.

- The verb *to be* is an **ordinary (main or principal) verb** and shows the existence of a person or thing, and gives information about a person or thing including occurence, identity, condition, state, quality and opinion:

    We *are* alive. (existence)

    Lunch *is* at noon. (occurence)

    Yesterday *was* Saturday. (identity)

    We *have been* very sick. (condition)

    She *can be* very difficult. (state)

    He *is being* kind. (quality)

    They *were* against smoking in public. (opinion)

- The verb *to be* is used to convey orders, destiny, etc. I *am to go*. He *is to stay* here.
- The verb *to be* is an **irregular verb**: *be, being, been; am, is are; was, were.*
- The verb *to be* is an **intransitive verb**. It has no object, but often has a complement:

A noun phrase:	She **is** a *talented dancer.*
An adjective:	The flowers **are** *beautiful*.
A preposition phrase:	The children **were** *on the lawn*.
An adverb:	Their mother **was** *nearby*.

    Note: A *preposition phrase* or an *adverb* can be called an *adverbial*.

- The verb *to be* is a **plain auxiliary verb** and is used to form tenses:

Present continuous:	I *am going*. (He/she/it *is going*. We/you/they *are going*.)
Present perfect continuous:	I *have been going*. (He/she/it *has been going*.)
Past continuous:	I/He/She/It *was going*. (We/you/they *were going*.)
Past perfect continuous:	I *had been going*. (for all persons)
Future continuous:	I *will be going*. (for all persons)
Future perfect continuous:	I *will have been going*. (for all persons)

- The verb *to be* is used to form **passive verb forms**. See Passive Verb Forms on pages 69-71.

    Note: For contractions or verbs, see Contractions in Chapter 3 on pages 114-116.

The following tables contain the past, present and future tenses of the verb *to be* as an active verb.

TABLE 2.6 Present tenses of the verb *to be* as an active verb

Present simple	Present continuous	Present perfect	Present perfect continuous
Statement	**Statement**	**Statement**	**Statement**
I am a mother.	I am being kind.	I have been to work.	I have been being silly.*
You are a mother.	You are being kind.	You have been to work.	
She is a mother.	He is being kind.	She has been to work.	
We are mothers.	We are being kind.	We have been to work.	
You are mothers.	You are being kind.	You have been to work.	
They are mothers.	They are being kind.	They have been to work.	
Negative	**Negative**	**Negative**	**Negative**
I am not a mother.	I am not being kind.	I have not been to work.	I have not been being silly.*
You are not a mother.	You are not being kind.	You have not been to work.	
She is not a mother.	He is not being kind.	She has not been to work.	
We are not mothers.	We are not being kind.	We have not been to work.	
You are not mothers.	You are not being kind.	You have not been to work.	
They are not mothers.	They are not being kind.	They have not been to work.	
Question	**Question**	**Question**	**Question**
Am I a mother?	Am I being kind?	Have I been to work?	Have you been being silly?*
Are you a mother?	Are you being kind?	Have you been to work?	
Is she a mother?	Is she being kind?	Has she been to work?	
Are we mothers?	Are we being kind?	Have we been to work?	
Are you mothers?	Are you being kind?	Have you been to work?	
Are they mothers?	Are they being kind?	Have they been to work?	

* These sentences are grammatically correct, but are not often used, because they sound clumsy.

TABLE 2.7 Past tenses of the verb *to be* as an active verb

Past simple	Past continuous	Past perfect	Past perfect continuous
Statement	**Statement**	**Statement**	**Statement**
I was a teacher.	I was being funny.	I had been to school.	I had been being naughty.*
You were a teacher.	You were being funny.	You had been to school.	
He was a teacher.	She was being funny.	She had been to school.	
We were teachers.	We were being funny.	We had been to school.	
You were teachers.	You were being funny.	You had been to school.	
They were teachers.	They were being funny.	They had been to school.	
Negative	**Negative**	**Negative**	**Negative**
I was not a teacher.	I was not being funny.	I had not been to school.	I had not been being naughty.*
You were not a teacher.	You were not being funny.	You had not been to school.	
He was not a teacher.	He was not being funny.	He had not been to school.	
We were not teachers.	We were not being funny.	We had not been to school.	
You were not teachers.	You were not being funny.	You had not been to school.	
They were not teachers.	They were not being funny.	They had not been to school.	
Question	**Question**	**Question**	**Question**
Was I a teacher?	Was I being funny?	Had I been to school?	Had you been being naughty?*
Were you a teacher?	Were you being funny?	Had you been to school?	
Was she a teacher?	Was she being funny?	Had she been to school?	
Were we teachers?	Were we being funny?	Had we been to school?	
Were you teachers?	Were you being funny?	Had you been to school?	
Were they teachers?	Were they being funny?	Had they been to school?	

* These sentences are grammatically correct, but are not often used, because they sound clumsy.

TABLE 2.8 Future tenses of the verb *to be* as an active verb

Future simple	Future continuous	Future perfect	Future perfect continuous
Statement	**Statement**	**Statement**	**Statement**
I will be famous.	I will be being helpful if I do that job.*	I will have been to the park.	I will have been being interviewed for 2 hours by then.*
You will be famous.		You will have been to the park.	
She will be famous.		She will have been to the park.	
We will be famous.		We will have been to the park.	
You will be famous.		You will have been to the park.	
They will be famous.		They will have been to the park.	
Negative	**Negative**	**Negative**	**Negative**
I will not be famous.	I will not be being helpful if I do that job.*	I will not have been to the park.	I will not have been being interviewed for 2 hours by then.*
You will not be famous.		You will not have been to the park.	
He will not be famous.		She will not have been to the park.	
We will not be famous.		We will not have been to the park.	
You will not be famous.		You will not have been to the park.	
They will not be famous.		They will not have been to the park.	
Question	**Question**	**Question**	**Question**
Will I be famous?	Will I be being helpful if I do that job?*	Will I have been to the park?	Will I have been being interviewed for 2 hours by then?
Will you be famous?		Will you have been to the park?	
Will she be famous?		Will he have been to the park?	
Will we be famous?		Will we have been to the park?	
Will you be famous?		Will you have been to the park?	
Will they be famous?		Will they have been to the park?	

* These sentences are grammatically correct, but are not often used, because they sound clumsy.

The verb *to have*

The verb *to have* is an important verb in the English language.

- The verb *to have* is an **ordinary (main or principal) verb** and shows possession or ownership; experience of something; getting something done; and describes actions.

    They *have* two dogs. (possession)

    We *had* our tickets *stolen* before we arrived at the game. (experience of something)

    I *will have* this suit dry cleaned. (getting something done)

    He *has played* very well. (describes actions)

- The verb *to have* is an **irregular verb** – *have, has, had*.

- The verb *to have* is a **transitive verb** and takes a direct object.

    We *have* a lovely *family*.

- The verb *to have* is a **plain auxiliary verb** and is used to form tenses:

    Present perfect: I *have looked* at the book. (he/she/it *has*)

    Present perfect continuous: I *have been looking* at the book. (he/she/it *has*)

    Past perfect: I *had looked* at the book before I bought it.

    Past perfect continuous: I *had been looking* at the book before I decided to buy it.

    Future perfect: I *will have looked* at the book by the time my friends arrive.

    Future perfect continuous: I *will have been looking* at the book by then.

    Perfect conditional: I *would have looked* at the book if I'd known about it.

    Perfect conditional continuous: I *would have been looking* at the book then.

- The verb *to have* plus the infinitive is used to express obligation:

    I *have to learn* English. I *have to go* to the doctor.

- The verb *to have* plus *got* (is used informally for possession or acquisition):

    She *has got* a baby. The baby *has got* a dummy.

- Interrogative (question):

    Do you *have* a baby? (normal English)

    Have you *got* a baby? (informal English)

    Have you a baby? (formal English)

    Note: For contractions of verbs see Contractions in Chapter 3 pages 114-116.

The following tables contain the past, present and future tenses of the verb *to have* as an active verb.

TABLE 2.9 Present tenses of the verb *to have* as an active verb

Present simple	Present continuous	Present perfect	Present perfect continuous
Statement	Statement	Statement	Statement
I have a dog.	I am having coffee.	I have had a holiday.	I have been having a sleep.
You have a dog.	You are having coffee.	You have had a holiday.	You have been having a sleep.
She has a dog.	She is having coffee.	He has had a holiday.	He has been having a sleep.
We have a dog.	We are having coffee.	We have had a holiday.	We have been having a sleep.
You have a dog.	You are having coffee.	You have had a holiday.	You have been having a sleep.
They have a dog.	They are having coffee.	They have had a holiday.	They have been having a sleep.
Negative	Negative	Negative	Negative
I do not have a dog.	I am not having coffee.	I have not had a holiday.	I have not been having a sleep.
You do not have a dog.	You are not having coffee.	You have not had a holiday.	You have not been having a sleep.
He does not have a dog.	He is not having coffee.	She has not had a holiday.	He has not been having a sleep.
We do not have a dog.	We are not having coffee.	We have not had a holiday.	We have not been having a sleep.
You do not have a dog.	You are not having coffee.	You have not had a holiday.	You have not been having a sleep.
They do not have a dog.	They are not having coffee.	They have not had a holiday.	They have not been having a sleep.
Question	Question	Question	Question
Do I have a dog?	Am I having coffee?	Have I had a holiday?	Have I been having a sleep?
Do you have a dog?	Are you having coffee?	Have you had a holiday?	Have you been having a sleep?
Does she have a dog?	Is he having coffee?	Has she had a holiday?	Has she been having a sleep?
Do we have a dog?	Are we having coffee?	Have we had a holiday?	Have we been having a sleep?
Do you have a dog?	Are you having coffee?	Have you had a holiday?	Have you been having a sleep?
Do they have a dog?	Are they having coffee?	Have they had a holiday?	Have they been having a sleep?

TABLE 2.10 Past tenses of the verb *to have* as an active verb

Past simple	Past continuous	Past perfect	Past perfect continuous
Statement	**Statement**	**Statement**	**Statement**
I had a car.	I was having a run.	I had had a party.	I had been having breakfast.
You had a car.	You were having a run.	You had had a party.	You had been having breakfast.
He had a car.	He was having a run.	He had had a party.	He had been having breakfast.
We had a car.	We were having a run.	We had had a party.	We had been having breakfast.
You had a car.	You were having a run.	You had had a party.	You had been having breakfast.
They had a car.	They were having a run.	They had had a party.	They had been having breakfast.
Negative	**Negative**	**Negative**	**Negative**
I did not have a car.	I was not having a run.	I had not had a party.	I had not been having breakfast.
You did not have a car.	You were not having a run.	You had not had a party.	You had not been having breakfast.
She did not have a car.	He was not having a run.	He had not had a party.	He had not been having breakfast.
We did not have a car.	We were not having a run.	We had not had a party.	We had not been having breakfast.
You did not have a car.	You were not having a run.	You had not had a party.	You had not been having breakfast.
They did not have a car.	They were not having a run.	They had not had a party.	They had not been having breakfast.
Question	**Question**	**Question**	**Question**
Did I have a car?	Was I having a run?	Had I had a party?	Had I been having breakfast?
Did you have a car?	Were you having a run?	Had you had a party?	Had you been having breakfast?
Did she have a car?	Was he having a run?	Had she had a party?	Had he been having breakfast?
Did we have a car?	Were we having a run?	Had we had a party?	Had we been having breakfast?
Did you have a car?	Were you having a run?	Had you had a party?	Had you been having breakfast?
Did they have a car?	Were they having a run?	Had they had a party?	Had they been having breakfast?

TABLE 2.11 Future tenses of the verb *to have* as an active verb

Future simple	Future continuous	Future perfect	Future perfect continuous
Statement	**Statement**	**Statement**	**Statement**
I will have lunch.	I will be having a baby.	I will have had some.	I will have been having tea.
You will have lunch.	You will be having a baby.	You will have had some.	You will have been having tea.
He will have lunch.	She will be having a baby.	She will have had some.	He will have been having tea.
We will have lunch.	We will be having a baby.	We will have had some.	We will have been having tea.
You will have lunch.	You will be having a baby.	You will have had some.	You will have been having tea.
They will have lunch.	They will be having a baby.	They will have had some.	They will have been having tea.
Negative	**Negative**	**Negative**	**Negative**
I will not have lunch.	I will not be having a baby.	I will not have had any.	I will not have been having tea.
You will not have lunch.	You will not be having a baby.	You will not have had any.	You will not have been having tea.
He will not have lunch.	She will not be having a baby.	She will not have had any.	He will not have been having tea.
We will not have lunch.	We will not be having a baby.	We will not have had any.	We will not have been having tea.
You will not have lunch.	You will not be having a baby.	You will not have had any.	You will not have been having tea.
They will not have lunch.	They will not be having a baby.	They will not have had any.	They will not have been having tea.
Question	**Question**	**Question**	**Question**
Will I have lunch?	Will I be having a baby?	Will I have had some?	Will I have been having tea?
Will you have lunch?	Will you be having a baby?	Will you have had some?	Will you have been having tea?
Will he have lunch?	Will she be having a baby?	Will she have had some?	Will he have been having tea?
Will we have lunch?	Will we be having a baby?	Will we have had some?	Will we have been having tea?
Will you have lunch?	Will you be having a baby?	Will you have had some?	Will you have been having tea?
Will they have lunch?	Will they be having a baby?	Will they have had some?	Will they have been having tea?

The verb *to do*

The verb *to do* is an important verb in the English language.

- The verb *to do* is an **ordinary (main or principal) verb** and is used for actions such as performing, carrying out, achieving or completing work.

    Nate is now *doing* another show. (performing)

    The ballet teachers *have done* a wonderful job with the students. (achieving)

    The students *did* the work. (completing)

- The verb *to do* is an **irregular verb** – do, does, did, done.

- The verb *to do* is a **transitive verb** and takes a direct object.

    She's doing her *homework*.

- The verb *to do* is a **plain auxiliary verb** and is used to form the negative and interrogative of the present simple and past simple tenses.

Present simple (negative):	We *do not work*. (We *don't work*.)
	She *does not work*. (She *doesn't work*.)
Present simple (question):	*Do* they *work*?
	Does he *work*?
Past simple (negative):	I *did not work*. (I *didn't work*)
Past simple (question):	*Did* you *work*?

- *Do* and *did* plus the infinitive without *to* can add stress to speech.

    He *does mean* what he says. (instead of: He means what he says.)

    I *did see* that man steal the money. (instead of: I saw that man steal the money.)

- *Do* is used to avoid repetition in dialogue:

Monica cooks very well.	Yes, she *does*.
Your friend danced very well.	Yes, she *did*.
Did you go to work today?	No, I *didn't*.

- *Do* is used after an introduction:

This is my friend Monica.	How *do* you *do*?

    Note: For contractions of verbs see Contractions in Chapter 3, pages 114-116.

The following tables contain the past, present and future tenses of the verb *to do* as an active verb.

TABLE 2.12 Present tenses of the verb *to do* as an active verb

Present simple	Present continuous	Present perfect	Present perfect continuous
Statement	**Statement**	**Statement**	**Statement**
I do my hair.	I am doing a task.	I have done my work.	I have been doing a project.
You do your hair.	You are doing a task.	You have done your work.	You have been doing a a project.
He does his hair.	She is doing a task.	He has done his work.	He has been doing a project.
We do our hair.	We are doing a task.	We have done our work.	We have been doing a project.
You do your hair.	You are doing a task.	You have done your work.	You have been doing a project.
They do their hair.	They are doing a task.	They have done their work.	They have been doing a project.
Negative	**Negative**	**Negative**	**Negative**
I do not do my hair.	I am not doing a task.	I have not done my work.	I have not been doing a project.
You do not do your hair.	You are not doing a task.	You have not done your work.	You have not been doing a project.
She does not do her hair.	He is not doing a task.	He has not done his work.	She has not been doing a project.
We do not do our hair.	We are not doing a task.	We have not done our work.	We have not been doing a project.
You do not do your hair.	You are not doing a task.	You have not done your work.	You have not been doing a project.
They do not do their hair.	They are not doing a task.	They have not done their work.	They have not been doing a project.
Question	**Question**	**Question**	**Question**
Do I do my hair?	Am I doing a task?	Have I done my work?	Have I been doing a project?
Do you do your hair?	Are you doing a task?	Have you done your work?	Have you been doing a project?
Does he do his hair?	Is she doing a task?	Has she done her work?	Has she been doing a project?
Do we do our hair?	Are we doing a task?	Have we done our work?	Have we been doing a project?
Do you do your hair?	Are you doing a task?	Have you done your work?	Have you been doing a project?
Do they do their hair?	Are they doing a task?	Have they done their work?	Have they been doing a project?

TABLE 2.13 Past tenses of the verb *to do* as an active verb

Past simple	Past continuous	Past perfect	Past perfect continuous
Statement	**Statement**	**Statement**	**Statement**
I did my best.	I was doing chores.	I had done the dishes.	I had been doing the washing.
You did your best.	You were doing chores.	You had done the dishes.	You had been doing the washing.
He did his best.	He was doing chores.	He had done the dishes.	She had been doing the washing.
We did our best.	We were doing chores.	We had done the dishes.	We had been doing the washing.
You did your best.	You were doing chores.	You had done the dishes.	You had been doing the washing.
They did their best.	They were doing chores.	They had done the dishes.	They had been doing the washing.
Negative	**Negative**	**Negative**	**Negative**
I did not do my best.	I was not doing chores.	I had not done the dishes.	I had not been doing the washing.
You did not do your best.	You were not doing chores.	You had not done the dishes.	You had not been doing the washing.
She did not do her best.	He was not doing chores.	She had not done the dishes.	He had not been doing the washing.
We did not do our best.	We were not doing chores.	We had not done the dishes.	We had not been doing the washing.
You did not do your best.	You were not doing chores.	You had not done the dishes.	You had not been doing the washing.
They did not do their best.	They were not doing chores.	They had not done the dishes.	They had not been doing the washing.
Question	**Question**	**Question**	**Question**
Did I do my best?	Was I doing chores?	Had I done the dishes?	Had I been doing the washing?
Did you do your best?	Were you doing chores?	Had you done the dishes?	Had you been doing the washing?
Did she do her best?	Was he doing chores?	Had she done the dishes?	Had he been doing the washing?
Did we do our best?	Were we doing chores?	Had we done the dishes?	Had we been doing the washing?
Did you do your best?	Were you doing chores?	Had you done the dishes?	Had you been doing the washing?
Did they do their best?	Were they doing chores?	Had they done the dishes?	Had they been doing the washing?

TABLE 2.14 Future tenses of the verb *to do* as an active verb

Future simple	Future continuous	Future perfect	Future perfect continuous
Statement	**Statement**	**Statement**	**Statement**
I will do that.	I will be doing homework.	I will have done it.	I will have been doing too much.
You will do that.	You will be doing homework.	You will have done it.	You will have been doing too much.
He will do that.	He will be doing homework.	She will have done it.	He will have been doing too much.
We will do that.	We will be doing homework.	We will have done it.	We will have been doing too much.
You will do that.	You will be doing homework.	You will have done it.	You will have been doing too much.
They will do that.	They will be doing homework.	They will have done it.	They will have been doing too much.
Negative	**Negative**	**Negative**	**Negative**
I will not do that.	I will not be doing homework.	I will not have done it.	I will not have been doing too much.
You will not do that.	You will not be doing homework.	You will not have done it.	You will not have been doing too much.
She will not do that.	He will not be doing homework.	She will not have done it.	He will not have been doing too much.
We will not do that.	We will not be doing homework.	We will not have done it.	We will not have been doing too much.
You will not do that.	You will not be doing homework.	You will not have done it.	You will not have been doing too much.
They will not do that.	They will not be doing homework.	They will not have done it.	They will not have been doing too much.
Question	**Question**	**Question**	**Question**
Will I do that?	Will I be doing homework?	Will I have done it?	Will I have been doing too much?
Will you do that?	Will you be doing homework?	Will you have done it?	Will you have been doing too much?
Will he do that?	Will she be doing homework?	Will he have done it?	Will she have been doing too much?
Will we do that?	Will we be doing homework?	Will we have done it?	Will we have been doing too much?
Will you do that?	Will you be doing homework?	Will you have done it?	Will you have been doing too much?
Will they do that?	Will they be doing homework?	Will they have done it?	Will they have been doing too much?

ADVERBS

An adverb is a word that modifies some parts of speech, but does NOT modify a noun or a pronoun.

USE OF ADVERBS

> Adverbs mainly express how, when, where, how often and how much.
> Adverbs mainly modify a verb, but can also modify an adjective or another adverb.

He walks *slowly*. (verb: to walk)

She is a *very* pretty girl. (adjective: pretty)

The wind blew *quite* suddenly. (adverb: suddenly)

TYPES OF ADVERBS

1. **HOW (MANNER)**: *quickly, bravely, well, slowly, suddenly, happily, fast, eagerly, anxiously, hard, carefully, angrily, badly, nicely, noisily, quietly.*

   He *carefully* opened the package. (how)

2. **WHEN (TIME)**: *today, now, yet, then, soon, yesterday, still, once, afterwards, eventually, daily, weekly, finally, before, already, last year.*

   I went to work *yesterday*. (when)

3. **WHERE (PLACE)**: *here, up, down, there, upstairs, near, outside, by, nearby.*

   The boy went *outside*. (where)

4. **HOW OFTEN (FREQUENCY)**: *twice, sometimes, often, always, never, usually, ever, occasionally.*

   You are *always* in a hurry. (number or how often)

5. **HOW MUCH (DEGREE)**: *fairly, very, quite, rather, almost, completely, fully, hardly, too, really, enough, maybe, practically, nearly, partly, sort of, scarcely.*

   It was *very* cold. (extent)

6. **SENTENCE**: *surely, certainly, definitely, probably, obviously, clearly, luckily, unfortunately, fortunately, undoubtedly.*

   I will *definitely* be going to the movies. (certainty)

   Note: Sentence adverbs modify the whole sentence or clause and normally express the speaker's opinion. They can be in any position – front position is mainly used.

7 **INTERROGATIVE**: *where, why, when, how.*

Why did you come? (question)

Note: Interrogative adverbs are placed at the beginning of a question.

8 **REASON**: *since, as, consequently, therefore.*

All the plants have flowered *since* it rained. (tells why)

9 **RELATIVE**: *where, when, why.*

James wanted to know *where* Carmelita had gone.

Note: Relative adverbs (also used as subordinating conjunctions) join two clauses and usually follow a verb asking for information. They are also used to introduce relative (adjective) clauses.

10 **SUBSTITUTE**: *yes, absolutely, no, never.*

These adverbs can replace a whole sentence.

   a **Affirmation**: *yes, absolutely.*

'Do you like ice-cream?' '*Yes!*' (I do like ice-cream.)

When somebody offers something, it is polite to add 'please'.

'Would you like an ice-cream?' '*Yes, please!*'

   b **Negation**: *no, never.*

'Are you going to work tomorrow?' '*No!*' (I'm not going to work tomorrow.)

When somebody offers something, it is polite to add 'thank you'.

'Do you need me to do anything for you?' '*No, thank you!*'

Note: *Not* is also used as an expression of negation, but cannot stand alone. It is used with auxiliary verbs – *have not, cannot* – or in a phrase – *not at all, not ever, certainly not.*

'We *have not* moved yet' (usually contracted to *haven't*)

'We *cannot* find a suitable place' (usually contracted to *can't*)

'Do you enjoy flying?'

'*Not at all!*' (I do not enjoy flying at all.)

For more information about *not*, see Contractions on pages 115-116.

POSITION OF ADVERBS

▶ Adverbs can be put at the beginning, middle, or end of a sentence.

Then the plane *suddenly* began to descend *rapidly*.

Many adverbs can be placed in any of these positions.

a Beginning: the adverb is placed at the beginning of the sentence.

Occasionally they go to the movies.

b Middle: the adverb is placed between the auxiliary verb and the action verb.

They will *occasionally* go to the movies.

If there is no auxiliary verb, the adverb is placed before the main verb.

They *occasionally* go to the movies.

c End: the adverb is placed at the end of the sentence.

They go to the movies *occasionally*.

▶ Adverbs come after the verb *to be* when it is on its own.

He is *probably* correct.

▶ Adverbs are not usually placed between a verb and the direct object.

He plays music *passionately*. RIGHT

He plays *passionately* music. WRONG

However, adverbs can be placed before an extra long object.

He plays, *passionately*, music he has written himself.

Adverbs in questions

Where auxiliary verbs are used, adverbs are usually placed between the auxiliary verb and the action verb.

Do you *always* go to that restaurant?

Have you *ever* been to the snow?

Could you *quickly* find that book for me, please?

Position for adverbs of manner

Middle position or end position:

They *wisely* stopped for a rest. (middle)

The children played *happily*. (end)

Position for adverbs of place and time

Usually end position:

> Please go *outside*. (place)
>
> The family is coming *soon*. (time)

Position for adverbs of frequency

Usually middle position:

> Do you *always* prefer coffee to tea?
>
> I can *sometimes* hear the birds singing.

Sentence adverbs

Any position, but usually the beginning of the sentence:

> *Unfortunately* they didn't have any money.
>
> They *obviously* weren't home.

ADVERBS FORMED FROM ADJECTIVES

Many adverbs, especially adverbs of manner and degree, are formed by adding *-ly* to an adjective.

▸ Adverb of manner: *slowly* (adjective: slow)

> The drivers had a *slow* start. (adjective)
>
> The drivers started *slowly*. (adverb)

▸ Adverb of degree: *completely* (adjective: complete)

> It was a *complete* disaster. (adjective)
>
> It was *completely* disastrous. (adverb)

Some examples:

> The athletes ran *quickly*. (quick-ly)
>
> The people who watched were *really* impressed. (real-ly)
>
> He *carefully* carried his baby. (careful-ly)
>
> *Suddenly* the music stopped. (sudden-ly)
>
> We reached the harbour *safely*. (safe-ly)
>
> They *politely* asked us to leave. (polite-ly)
>
> I don't *normally* worry about things. (normal-ly)
>
> The father spoke *softly* to the child. (soft-ly)

Other spelling rules to make an adjective into an adverb:

1. **-y to -ily**:

heavy (adjective)	heavily (adverb)
lucky (adjective)	luckily (adverb)
happy (adjective)	happily (adverb)
easy (adjective)	easily (adverb)

2. **-le to -ly**:

reasonable (adjective)	reasonably (adverb)
incredible (adjective)	incredibly (adverb)
possible (adjective)	possibly (adverb)
probable (adjective)	probably (adverb)
sensible (adjective)	sensibly (adverb)
comfortable (adjective)	comfortably (adverb)
terrible (adjective)	terribly (adverb)

ADVERB PHRASES AND CLAUSES

➤ Adverb phrases contain a group of words that do the work of an adverb and do not contain a verb.

Ben swims *like a fish*.

If there is a single adverb and an adverb phrase in the end position in a sentence, usually the single adverb is placed first.

Ben swims *fast*, *like a fish*.

Note: Adverb phrases usually cannot go in the middle position.

Josh ate dinner *in a hurry*. RIGHT

Josh *in a hurry* ate dinner. WRONG

➤ Adverb clauses are dependent clauses that contain a group of words that do the work of an adverb and include a verb. They are introduced by an adverb or a subordinating conjunction.

Ben swims <u>when the season starts</u>. (time)

Josh goes to the beach <u>as he enjoys surfing</u>. (reason)

Rachel will succeed, <u>because she works hard</u>. (reason)

<u>Everywhere she goes</u>, people love her. (place)

SOME MORE ADVERBS FOR YOU TO USE

Adverbs ending with -ly (formed from adjectives)

absolutely	dramatically	heavily	passionately	scarcely
angrily	dreadfully	incredibly	politely	sensibly
anxiously	eagerly	loudly	possibly	slowly
badly	easily	luckily	practically	softly
bravely	enthusiastically	mainly	probably	suddenly
carefully	eventually	nearly	quickly	surely
certainly	fairly	nicely	quietly	technically
clearly	finally	noisily	rapidly	terribly
comfortably	fortunately	normally	really	undoubtedly
completely	fully	obviously	reasonably	unfortunately
consequently	happily	occasionally	recently	usually
definitely	hardly	partly	safely	vastly

Other adverbs

afterwards	even	next	sometimes	upstairs
again	ever	no	soon	very
almost	fast	not	still	weekly
already	hard	now	then	well
also	here	often	there	when
always	how	once	therefore	whenever
as	inside	only	today	where
before	just	outside	together	wherever
by	maybe	quite	tomorrow	why
daily	near	rather	too	yes
down	nearby	seldom	twice	yesterday
downstairs	never	since	up	yet

Note: Some adverbs may be used as prepositions or conjunctions.

1. Look at adverbs of place – *up, down, near* and *by*. These words can be used as adverbs or prepositions.

   Up:

   Adverb: He jumped *up* in the air. (to a higher place)

   Preposition: John climbed *up* the ladder. (position)

   Down:

   Adverb: The child fell *down*. (to a lower place)

   Preposition: Mark walked *down* the road. (position)

   Near:

   Adverb: The car drew *near* to them. (closer place)

   Preposition: Lauren sat *near* the TV. (position)

   By:

   Adverb: The soldiers marched *by*. (place)

   Preposition: Leanne stood *by* the door. (position)

2. Look at adverbs of time, such as *since*. These also can be used as prepositions or conjunctions:

   Adverb: The dead tree has *since* been cut down.

   Preposition: The greatest invention *since* the wheel.

   Conjunction: What have you been doing *since* we left the room?

For examples of adverbial conjunctions see Conjunctions on pages 96-98.

CONJUNCTIONS

A conjunction is a word that joins words, phrases or clauses in a sentence. Conjunctions are sometimes called linking words or connectors.

USE OF CONJUNCTIONS

➤ A conjunction is used **only** for joining words, phrases or clauses in a sentence.

salt *and* pepper. (words)

in the pool *or* at the beach. (phrases)

Mahira will go to the beach, *but* she will not swim. (clauses)

➤ A conjunction does not qualify a word.
➤ Conjunctions are used to make sentences longer and more interesting.
➤ Some conjunctions can be placed at the beginning of a sentence.

Because I like you, I'll send you an invitation to my party.

Although she didn't know them, she paid for their meal.

Note: Some words used as conjunctions can also be used as adverbs and prepositions.

The concert was over *before* we arrived. (conjunction)

We have been to this town *before*. (adverb)

The bride and groom knelt *before* the altar. (preposition)

TYPES OF CONJUNCTIONS

1 **Coordinating conjunctions** join words, phrases or clauses of equal rank in sentences: *and, but, yet, so, for, or, either/or, neither/nor, only, whereas*.

Jeanie will go to the beach *and* she will have a swim. (independent clauses of equal rank).

2 **Subordinating conjunctions** join clauses where one clause is the main clause and the other clause depends on it: *since, because, if, although, after, where, unless, before, consequently, as, until*.

Anne will go to the beach *if* you drive her.

3 **Adverbial conjunctions** are adverbs that are used as conjunctions and join two clauses that are separated by a semicolon with a comma after the adverbial conjunction: *however, otherwise, therefore, finally, nevertheless, meanwhile, besides*.

Brian broke his leg; *therefore*, he couldn't drive the car.

CONJUNCTION PHRASES AND CLAUSES

➤ A **conjunction phrase** does the work of a conjunction and ends in a simple conjunction: *as if, as soon as, as well as, even though, in order that*.

We are tired *as well as* hungry.

He took a bus *in order that* he might see the city.

➤ A **conjunction clause** contains a coordinating, subordinating or adverbial conjunction: *and, but, because, since, however, therefore*.

They went to the shops <u>*and* they bought some groceries</u>.

I would love to go to the movies <u>*since* you have some tickets</u>.

They played very well; <u>*therefore*, they won the cup</u>.

MORE EXAMPLES OF COORDINATING CONJUNCTIONS

and	for	only	whereas
but	neither/nor	or	yet
either/or	now	so	

We went to the movies *and* I bought some popcorn.

Sue was born in South Africa, *but* she lives in Australia.

They can have *either* chocolate *or* ice-cream.

He didn't understand, *for* he didn't speak Italian.

I can eat *neither* chocolate *nor* ice-cream.

He can get a job, *now* that he has finished his Degree.

You can sleep where you like, *only* please don't snore.

Put some sun cream on your face *or* you will get very sun burnt.

I was hot *so* I had a drink.

James went to South America, *whereas* Nancy went to Malaysia.

Canada won the race, *yet* the favourite team was the USA.

MORE EXAMPLES OF SUBORDINATING CONJUNCTIONS

after	consequently	than	when
although	if	that	where
because	notwithstanding	though	while
before	since	unless	why

Although the baby was very tired, she smiled at us.

We had to catch the bus *because* it was raining.

We must go to the shops *before* it is too late.

I ate a very big lunch, *consequently* I'm not hungry.

You must evacuate the town *if* it begins to flood.

We haven't heard a sound *since* she fell asleep.

We laughed so much *that* our eyes watered.

Though/although he was late, he was able to catch the right train.

She started to cry *when* she heard the bad news about her friend.

We will keep working *while* it is light.

She can't read *unless* she wears glasses.

MORE EXAMPLES OF ADVERBIAL CONJUNCTIONS

accordingly	furthermore	moreover	still
also	however	namely	then
anyway	incidentally	nevertheless	thereafter
besides	indeed	next	therefore
certainly	instead	nonetheless	thus
finally	likewise	otherwise	undoubtedly
further	meanwhile	similarly	

She stayed at home today; *besides*, she felt ill.

We won the last game; *finally*, we had the championship cup!

He lost his wallet; *however*, the police found it.

We couldn't get tickets to the movie; *instead*, we went for a walk.

He was running very late; *nevertheless*, he caught the train on time.

They didn't win the match; *nonetheless*, they enjoyed the day.

I will drive to town; *otherwise*, I'll be late for work.

We ran out of petrol and had to walk home; *still*, we had a great day at the beach.

We watched TV until very late; *then*, we remembered that we had to get up early.

I've finished my course; *therefore*, I can get a job.

They loved their holiday; *undoubtedly*, they'll go again.

INTERJECTIONS

An interjection is a word or exclamation used to show strong feelings or emotions.

USE OF INTERJECTIONS

- Interjections are usually involuntary exclamations.
- Interjections are usually followed by an exclamation mark: !
- Interjections are mainly used in dialogue.

'*Hurray*, we won the cup!' shouted the excited players.

TYPES OF INTERJECTIONS

1 Sounds that naturally express feelings: *Ah!, Phew!, Oh!, Ha!, Hurrah!, Wow!, Whoa!, Hey!, Yay!*

'*Wow*! What a fabulous view!'

'*Hey*! How are you?'

'*Oh*! What a disaster!'

2 Phrases that have been reduced and the original meanings have gone: *Good grief!, Hello!, Goodbye!, Alas!, Hear! Hear!, Bravo!*

'*Bravo*! An amazing performance!'

'*Hello*! How are you?'

'*Hear! Hear*! Well said!'

'*Goodbye*! I'll see you later.'

'*Alas*! We couldn't find the money!'

Interjection phrases are extended interjections:

'*My goodness!*'

'*Wow, what a catch!*'

'*How wonderful!*'

'*Oh, bad luck!*'

CHAPTER 3
PUTTING IT TOGETHER

Sentences

Phrases and clauses

Questions in conversation (dialogue)

Direct and indirect (reported) speech

Contractions

Punctuation

Now that you have the basic understanding of grammar, it's time to put what you've learned into practice.

SENTENCES

English writing (and speech) is made up of sentences. They are words put into a particular pattern using the parts of speech in phrases and clauses.

> Sentences can take the forms of statements, questions, commands or exclamations.

May drinks her milk every day. (statement)

Does May drink milk every day? (question)

Drink your milk please, May. (command)

You're a good girl! (exclamation)

> Every sentence must have, at least, a subject and a predicate (verb).

The smallest sentence in the English language is: 'I am.' (I exist.) However, most sentences are longer that *I am* and contain phrases and/or clauses to make them more interesting and informative.

> Sentences are grouped together to form paragraphs. Each sentence in the paragraph expresses a complete thought, while each paragraph discusses an individual point or topic.

Note: Do not use too many long, complicated sentences, as they can be hard to write and read. Short sentences can produce dramatic effect or tension in your writing.

The lights went out! The movie began!

PARTS OF A SENTENCE

1 **Subject**: the main noun or pronoun that tells who or what the sentence is about.

   Mike bought a new car. (subject: *Mike*)

2 **Predicate**: the verb and other parts of the sentence (including the object, complement and so on).

   Mike *bought a new car*. (predicate: *bought a new car*)

   Complement: some transitive verbs need something more than the object to make the sentence complete:

   The children made me *smile*. (object: me; complement: smile)

   The subject can include more than one noun or pronoun:

   Brian and *Jan* bought a new house. (nouns)

   He and *I* went to the movies. (pronouns)

   The subject may be implied in command sentences:

   Open the window, please! (*you* is the subject and is implied)

TYPES OF SENTENCES

Simple sentences:

➤ Simple sentences contain a subject, a verb and an object (and can also be called independent clauses in a longer sentence).

   Tim went home.

   Tim is the subject, *went* is the verb, *home* is the object.

➤ Simple sentences can be more complicated:

   The boy went to the movies.

   We have now included a preposition phrase *to the movies*.

➤ Simple sentences can also include adjectives, adverbs and simple phrases:

   The young boy waited eagerly in the theatre to see his favourite movie.

   Young and *favourite* are adjectives and *eagerly* is an adverb.

   The young boy, *waited eagerly*, *in the theatre*, and *to see his favourite movie* are all simple phrases.

Compound sentences

➤ Compound sentences include at least two independent clauses joined by a coordinating conjunction:

I play tennis regularly and *I am really fit*.

➤ Compound sentences can also be joined by an adverbial conjunction. The first clause ends with a semicolon and there is a comma after the adverbial conjunction.

Brian broke his leg; *therefore*, he couldn't drive the car.

Complex sentences

➤ Complex sentences include an independent clause and one or more dependent clauses. There are three types of dependent clauses used in complex sentences:

1 ADVERB CLAUSE

The young boy went to the theatre because he had a ticket.

The young boy went to the theatre (is the independent clause)

he had a ticket (is the dependent **adverb** clause joined by the subordinating conjunction *because*).

2 ADJECTIVE (RELATIVE) CLAUSE

The young boy who had paid for his ticket waited eagerly in the theatre.

*The young boy waited eagerly in the theatre (*is the independent clause)

who had paid for his ticket (is the dependent **adjective** clause. It describes the boy.)

3 NOUN CLAUSE

The young boy was overjoyed that the movie was fantastic.

*The young boy was overjoyed (*is the independent clause)

that the movie was fantastic (is the dependent **noun** clause).

Positive and negative sentences

May drinks her milk every day. (positive statement)

May doesn't drink milk every day. (negative statement)

Does May drink milk every day? (positive question)

Doesn't May drink milk every day? (negative question)

Does May not drink milk every day? (negative emphatic question)

Drink your milk please, May. (positive command)

Don't drink that milk please, May. (negative command)

You're a good girl! (positive exclamation)

This milk is not cold enough! (negative exclamation)

PHRASES AND CLAUSES

> Phrases and clauses are the building blocks of sentences. Every sentence uses the parts of speech in phrases and clauses.

PHRASES

Phrases refer to a few words that go together to give a certain meaning in a sentence, but do not make a complete sentence on their own. They do not have a subject and a predicate (verb):

> on the beach, under the trees, very pretty, is working

A phrase can sometimes be just one word:

> *book* (noun phrase); *bad* (adjective phrase)

Types of phrases

1. **Adjective phrases** contain a group of words that describe something without a verb.

    Is she *really happy*?

2. **Adverb phrases** contain a group of words that do the work of an adverb and do not have a verb.

    Matthew walked *quite slowly*.

    Did John run *like the wind*?

3. **Conjunction phrases** do the work of a conjunction and usually end in a simple conjunction.

    She took a taxi *in order that* she might meet the train.

    Did John, *as well as* Jane, go to town?

4. **Interjection phrases** are phrases that have been reduced over time.

    Good grief! Wow!

5. **Noun phrases** are a group of words containing a noun, without a verb.

    English books are in the library.

    The bathroom looks fantastic!

6. **Preposition phrases** consist of a preposition plus a noun phrase, with no verb.

    Phillip and the team had drinks *under the trees*.

    Did Tim enjoy travelling *in the morning*?

7 **Verb phrases** contain a verb in various tenses.

Katrie *turned around* to see the screen.

She *is teaching* in a new school.

Participle phrases

A **participle** is an adjective that is formed from a verb and is used to modify a noun. Participles are sometimes called verbals (see note on page 43).

➤ Active verbs to participles (These participles are called present participles):

The magician *amazes* people. (active verb)

The *amazing* magician delights the people. (present participle)

The patient *annoyed* the doctor. (active verb)

The *annoying* patient went to the doctor. (present participle)

The trucks will *move* away later. (active verb)

The *moving* trucks were cheered by the crowd. (present participle)

➤ Passive verbs to participles (These participles are called past participles):

The child was *injured*. (passive verb)

The *injured* child was carried. (past participle)

The meal was *burned*. (passive verb)

The *burned* meal was awful. (past participle)

Her watch was *broken*. (passive verb)

Her *broken* watch will not work. (past participle)

Note: The terms 'present' and 'past' have nothing to do with present or past tense.

A **participle phrase** can be formed from a relative (adjective) clause or some adverb clauses. It includes a present or past participle and a noun. The entire phrase acts like an adjective in a sentence.

➤ Relative (adjective) clauses:

Jean, *who was an amazing French magician*, kept the crowd spellbound.

Mark, *who was loved by the crowd*, sang well.

Participle phrases formed from the above relative (adjective) clauses:

Jean, *the amazing French magician*, kept the crowd spellbound.

amazing = present participle, *magician* = noun

Mark, *loved by the crowd*, sang well.

loved = past participle, *crowd* = noun

- Adverb clauses:

    While he was shopping today, Mike found some great bargains.

    After he had cooked the meal, John sat down for a rest.

    Participle phrases formed from the above adverb clauses:

    While shopping today, Mike found some great bargains.

    shopping = present participle, *today* = noun

    Having cooked the meal, John sat down for a rest.

    having cooked = past participle, *meal* = noun

    Note: *Having* plus a past participle is called a **perfect participle**; it is used when one action is followed by another.

The second sentence in each pair of sentences below is an example of a participle phrase in a sentence.

Jenson, who looked tired, was put into his cot for a sleep.

Looking tired, Jenson was put into his cot for a sleep.

The new graduates who work at the university are from Japan.

The new graduates *working at the university* are from Japan.

The patients who were visited by that doctor were angry.

The patients *visited by that doctor* were angry.

The car was stolen by thieves and was damaged.

The car *stolen by thieves* was damaged.

Before they went for a swim, they checked the depth of the water.

Before going for a swim, they checked the depth of the water.

Since Laurie and Maree moved house, they have been very busy.

Since moving house, Laurie and Maree have been very busy.

Note: The subject is the same for a participle phrase as for the rest of the sentence.

Looking tired, Jenson was put into his cot for a sleep. (Jenson was tired)

Phrasal verbs

The following adverbs are sometimes used with a verb to make phrasal verbs and are mainly used in informal writing and speech: *out, off, down, back, in, on, up, round, forward, by, away, over, along, through.*

> We *get up* early in summer.
>
> Annie *drove off* and *ran over* a log.

➤ Some phrasal verbs have special meanings:

> When do we *take off*? (in a plane)
>
> The visitors finally *turned up*. (arrived late)

➤ Phrasal verbs plus a preposition:

> We *ran away from* the fire.
>
> Mike *took off from* Heathrow.

➤ Phrasal verb plus an object:

> I *turned off* the television.
>
> or
>
> I *turned the television off*.

➤ When using a pronoun:

> John *turned it* off. RIGHT
>
> John *turned off it*. WRONG

CLAUSES

A clause is a group of words with a subject and a verb. A clause is a sentence that is part of a larger sentence.

> I cannot find the book that you gave me.

➤ *I cannot find the book* is an independent clause or a main clause, and can stand on its own like a sentence.

➤ *that you gave me* is a dependent clause or a subordinate clause, and needs to be added to the independent clause for the sentence to make sense.

Types of clauses

1 **Adjective clauses (relative clauses)** are dependent clauses introduced by a relative pronoun or a relative adverb, which refer or relate to people or things in the independent clause. The adjective (relative) clause is placed directly after the noun or pronoun it describes or modifies.

➤ Relative pronouns: *who, whom, whose, which* and *that*.

➤ Relative adverbs: *where, when* and *why*.

There are three types of adjective (relative) clauses:

a Defining adjective (relative) clauses:

  The girl *who* served us is no longer in that shop.

  The pool *that* we swam in was huge.

  Carmelita hadn't been to the flat *where* James lived.

  They told us the reasons *why* they went away.

  There are no commas to isolate the clause from the rest of the sentence because the clause is needed to give clear understanding of the noun – e.g. *girl*.

b Non-defining adjective (relative) clauses:

  Aili, *who* went to Russia, bought this brooch for me.

  Jackie, to *whom* I was speaking, suddenly fainted.

  Jill, *whose* daughter was overseas, showed me photos of the family.

  August, *when* I was sick, was very cold.

  Commas are used to isolate the clause from the rest of the sentence, as the clause is not necessary to give clear understanding to the noun – e.g. *Aili*.

c Connective adjective (relative) clauses:

  Felicity sent a letter to Julie, *who* showed it to me.

  Our friend had triplets, two of *whom* were boys.

  We went to visit Julie, *whose* children were at home.

  Dad loved the present, *which* made him very happy.

  Commas are used to isolate the clause from the rest of the sentence, as the clause is not necessary to give clear understanding to the noun. These clauses are similar to non-defining adjective (relative) clauses, but are usually placed after the object of the main, active verb – e.g. *Julie*.

2. **Adverb clauses** are dependent clauses introduced by an adverb or a subordinating conjunction.

There are a number of types of adverb clauses:

   Manner: The huge plane suddenly shuddered *as if* it would break.
   Time: You mustn't use your phone *when you drive a vehicle*.
   Place: *Everywhere I go*, I meet people I know.
   Reason: All the plants have flowered, *because* it rained.

3. **Conjunction clauses** contain a coordinating, subordinating or adverbial conjunction: *and, but, because, since, however, therefore*.

   They went to the shops *and they bought some groceries*.

   I would love to go to the movies *since you have some tickets*.

   They played very well; *therefore, they won the cup*.

4. **Noun clauses** are dependent clauses that work like a noun, contain a verb and can be the subject, the object or the complement to a verb.

   What she did was very wrong. (subject)

   Where she is going nobody knows. (subject)

   I did not hear *what Jane said*. (object)

   They decided *that she was right*. (object)

   She did not believe *that he would go*. (object)

   They wanted to ask *if he would drive*. (object)

   They told him *that he had won*. (complement)

   The film was exactly *what we expected*. (complement)

5. **Relative clause**: see adjective clause.

   Note: In casual conversation it is sometimes acceptable to use phrases and clauses on their own. For example:

   'Where is Phillip?'

   '*Under the trees*.'

   and:

   'Will you get me a drink, please?'

   '*When you pay*!'

   'OK, I'll buy the drinks then.'

   '*Good grief*!'

QUESTIONS IN CONVERSATION (DIALOGUE)

Questions are mostly used in conversation (dialogue) to find out information.

SOME OF THE WAYS WE USE QUESTIONS

Suggesting: 'Shall we go on holidays, Ada?'

Asking permission: 'Could we go to Tasmania, Henk?'

Requesting: 'Would you drive us to the airport, please?'

Inviting: 'Would you like to walk on the beach, Jan?'

Offering: 'Can I help you, Bob?'

Asking for information: 'Do you know the time, please?'

TWO MAIN TYPES OF QUESTIONS

1 **Questions that only require 'yes' or 'no' answers:**

'Are you ok?' 'Yes.'

'Is it raining?' 'No.'

2 **Questions that start with *Wh-* and *How*:**

Who is he taking to the party?

What will you wear?

Which car will you drive?

Whose bag is this?

Where is the party?

When are the guests arriving?

Why didn't we go together?

How old is Aidan now?

AUXILIARY VERBS

The plain auxiliary verbs and modal (auxiliary) verbs go before the subject in a question.

> The **plain auxiliary verbs** are *be, have, do* and *will*.

> The **modal (auxiliary) verbs** are *can, could, may, might, must, will, would, shall* and *should*.

Use of plain auxiliary verbs and modal (auxiliary) verbs

Plain auxiliary verbs	**Modal (auxiliary) verbs**
Is it snowing?	*Can* you drive a car?
What *was* Jane sewing?	Where *should* I park the car?
Have you bought a new car?	What *would* you like to drink?
Had they served dinner?	*May* I borrow your pen, please?
Do you want a cup of coffee?	*Could* I have a cup of tea, please?
Will you go home?	Where *will* I meet you?

Note: When *do* is used as an auxiliary verb, the verb after the subject does not end with -*s* or –*ed*:

Why *does* she *like* that man?

Why *did* she *like* that man?

> Where more than one auxiliary verb is used, only the first one goes before the subject:

What *has* John *been* watching on television?

> Questions do not start with ordinary verbs such as *go*, *move* and *take*

When *goes* the bus? WRONG

When *does* the bus *go*? RIGHT

EXAMPLES OF QUESTIONS

Here are some questions and answers:

What's the weather like there? It's raining.

Where was Paul last night? Paul was at a dance.

When was she married? She was married three years ago.

What do you do in your spare time? I enjoy going to the movies.

Who wants to go to the beach? I'll go to the beach with you.

Here are some more examples of questions:

Where is Australia on the map?

What is the time?

Do you want to go to the movies?

Which of these two tables will you sit at?

Whose car have you borrowed?

How long will you be at the shops?

What is the purpose of the following questions?

Can I help you? (offering)

May I borrow your car please? (asking permission)

Could I have a cup of coffee please? (requesting)

Would you like to go out to dinner? (inviting)

Shall we take a taxi? (suggesting)

Do you have a map please? (asking for information)

Here are some examples of questions used in conversation (dialogue):

1 Very casual:

Mal:	'G'day Dave! How's it going?'
Dave:	'Couldn't be better, and you?'
Mal:	'Oh, OK. What are you doing these days?'
Dave:	'I'm enjoying retirement. What are you and Jill up to?'
Mal:	'Oh, travelling a bit. How's Judy?'
Dave:	'She's good thanks. When will you be down our way?'
Mal:	'We'll be there soon'

2 Friendly:

Lola:	'Hi, Wendy. How are you?'
Wendy:	'Really well thanks. It's good to see you, Lola. How are things?'
Lola:	'Great. It's been a long time, hasn't it?'
Wendy:	'Yes, too long. I've missed you heaps. Have you seen Bec at all?'
Lola:	'Yes. Can you and Peter come to dinner next week with Bec?'
Wendy:	'Sure! Which night?'
Lola:	'What about Friday at 6pm?'

3 More polite:

Jennifer:	'Hello John, how are you?'
John:	'I'm well thanks Jennifer. How are you?'
Jennifer:	'I'm very well thank you. It's good to see you. Have you seen Geoff?'
John:	'Yes. He'll be at the Reunion next week. Will you be there?'
Jennifer:	'Yes, I'm looking forward to meeting David and Clara again.'
John:	'I am too. Who else is going to be there?'
Jennifer:	'Well, Rose and Jackson said they might come.'

DIRECT AND INDIRECT (REPORTED) SPEECH

When we want to write down or say what somebody said, we can use either direct speech or indirect speech. Indirect speech can also be called reported speech.

DIRECT SPEECH

Direct speech is what a person actually said.

If we want to **write** those exact words, we put them into quotation marks (inverted commas):

Michelle said, 'I want you to meet Gary and April.'

If we want to **say** those exact words, we say:

Michelle said, *quote* I want you to meet Gary and April *unquote*.

INDIRECT (REPORTED) SPEECH

Indirect (reported) speech happens when we want to write down or say only the meaning of what was said:

Michelle said she wanted us to meet Gary and April.

➤ In indirect or reported speech we sometimes have to change the actual words:

'I *am* very happy.' (direct speech)

She *is* very happy. (indirect or reported speech)

➤ In indirect or reported speech we sometimes use *that*:

Michelle said *that* she wanted us to meet Gary and April.

She says *that* she is very happy.

➤ In indirect or reported speech the verb tense is usually changed:

'I *want* a good job.' (direct speech using present simple)

He *wanted* a good job. (indirect or reported speech using past simple)

Other examples of the verb tense changing:

Direct: Sara said, 'I *am dancing* tonight.' (present continuous)
Indirect: Sara said she *was dancing* tonight. (past continuous)

Direct:	Lynne said, 'She *has danced* well.' (present perfect)
Indirect:	Lynne said that she *had danced* well. (past perfect)
Direct:	Kevin said, 'I *loved* the ballet.' (past simple)
Indirect:	Kevin said that he *had loved* the ballet. (past perfect)
Direct:	Jan said, 'I *was writing* a letter.' (past continuous)
Indirect:	Jan said that she *had been writing* a letter. (past perfect continuous)
Direct:	Brian said, 'I *will have* a holiday.' (future simple)
Indirect:	Brian said that he *would have* a holiday. (present conditional)

➤ In some cases, the verb tense does not change:

Direct:	Marjo said, 'I *would love* to go.' (present conditional)
Indirect:	Marjo said that she *would love* to go. (present conditional)

➤ The verb tense does not need to change when something reported is still the same:

'I *am* very happy.' (direct speech: present simple)

She *is* very happy. (indirect or reported speech: present simple)

➤ For the *Wh-* and *How* questions (see Questions in this chapter), the verb changes and is also no longer in a question form:

Laurie asked, '*What are* you *drinking*, John?'

Laurie asked John *what* he *was drinking*.

Maree asked, '*How did* you *find* our new address?'

Maree asked us *how we found* their new address.

➤ For other questions the verb changes and *if* may be added:

John asked, '*Do* you *want* a drink, Laurie?'

John asked Laurie *if* he *wanted* a drink.

➤ Two verbs often used in indirect (or reported) speech are *tell* and *say*:

-*Tell* is used when we want to explain who is being spoken to:

Michelle *tells me* she's happy.

We *told them* they could stay with us.

-*Say* is used when we do not want to explain who is being spoken to:

Michelle *says* that she's happy.

We *said* they could stay with us.

CONTRACTIONS

A contraction is a shortened form of two joined words.

▸ When we shorten words we leave out some letters and use an apostrophe (') instead.
I've rung the doctor. (I have rung the doctor.)

▸ When a word is to be stressed, it cannot take the contracted form:
'Have you rung the doctor?' 'Yes, *I have*!'

▸ Contracted verbs following a pronoun are *be*, *have*, *would* and *will*.

I am	I'm
you are	you're
we are	we're
they are	they're
he is, he has	he's
she is, she has	she's
it is, it has	it's
I have	I've
you have	you've
we have	we've
they have	they've
I had, I would	I'd
you had, you would	you'd
he had, he would	he'd
she had, she would	she'd
it had, it would	it'd
we had, we would	we'd
they had, they would	they'd
I will	I'll
you will	you'll
he will	he'll
she will	she'll
it will	it'll
we will	we'll
they will	they'll

- Contractions can be placed after a noun:

    Edward's gone to see his friends. (Edward has gone)

    The *train'll* be really late. (The train will)

- Some verbs can be contracted after question words *why, what, when, where, who* and *how* and *here*, *there* and *that*:

    Why's she going home? (why is)

    What's he done with the keys? (what has)

    What'll happen to that boy? (what will)

    When's Mum going to town? (when is)

    Where'd you go today? (where did)

    Who's he talking to? (who is)

    Who'd want to go there? (who would)

    Who'll take the blame? (who will)

    How's your friend going? (how is)

    Here's your ticket. (here is)

    There'll be plenty of time. (there will)

    There'd be nothing left. (there would)

    That's not the right answer. (that is)

    That'd be nice. (that would)

- For negatives *not* becomes *n't*: for example *aren't (are not), isn't (is not), wasn't (was not), weren't (were not), haven't (have not), hasn't (has not), hadn't (had not), don't (do not), doesn't (does not), didn't (did not)*.

    Some more negative contractions:

    won't (will not)

    shan't (shall not)

    can't (cannot)

    couldn't (could not)

    mustn't (must not)

    needn't (need not)

    mightn't (might not)

    shouldn't (should not)

    wouldn't (would not)

    daren't (dare not)

In some cases either *not* or the verb can be contracted:

| It is not right. | It *isn't* right. | *It's* not right. |
| You will not go. | You *won't* go. | *You'll* not go. |

When contracted words are used in speech, they can be confusing for some people. Often they can only be understood when the meaning of the sentence is clear.

➤ *It is* can be contracted to *it's*:

It's a beautiful day. (It is a beautiful day.)

➤ *It has* can be contracted to *it's*:

It's become very cold. (It has become very cold.)

However, when we use the possessive adjective – *its* – we do not contract it.

The dog wagged *its* tail.

➤ *He is* can be contracted to *he's*:

He's my father. (He is my father.)

➤ *He has* can be contracted to *he's*:

He's bought a new car. (He has bought a new car.)

➤ *I had* can be contracted to *I'd*:

I'd taken the kids to school. (I had taken the kids to school.)

➤ *I would* can be contracted to *I'd*:

I'd love to go tonight. (I would love to go tonight.)

Note: One of the most common spelling mistakes is *your* for *you are* instead of *you're*. An easy way to remember which contraction to use is to sound out the sentence in your head without any contractions:

It's your turn. (It is your turn.)

You're next. (You are next.)

PUNCTUATION

Punctuation symbols are used to indicate the structure and organisation of written language to clarify meaning to the reader.

Punctuation is the most important process to ensure a reader understands your writing. Always check your work for correct punctuation. Not enough punctuation can leave the reader unsure of meaning, and too much punctuation can equally confuse. Also be sure you're using the correct punctuation. A misplaced comma can completely change the meaning of a sentence.

The following are the most common forms of punctuation and how to use them:

FULL STOP

A full stop is used to:

1 finish a sentence:

   We won the game.

2 show an abbreviation:

   P. Weaver

   Note: The modern tendency, however, is to omit the full stop in an abbreviation:

   P Weaver

COMMA

A comma is used to:

1 help the reader understand the meaning of the sentence:

   Can I please eat, Mum, before we go? RIGHT
   Can I please eat Mum before we go? WRONG

2 separate the words in a list:

   Monica bought carrots, beans, potatoes and onions.

3 include a short quotation:

   The teacher said, 'English is a very interesting subject.'

4 separate the name of a person from the rest of the sentence:

   Would you like to go to the movies with me, Jane?
   I think, Miss Weaver, that I would like to buy one of your famous teddy bears.

5 include phrases in the middle of a sentence:

Many drivers, especially on country roads, get very tired after a few hours.

6 separate participle phrases in a sentence:

<u>Hoping to win the match</u>, Phillip bowled the last over.

7 include an explanation about the subject (non-defining relative/adjective clause):

Merryn, who is a wonderful chef, is going to cook dinner for the family.

8 separate the day and year in a date:

February 22, 1945

22 February, 1945

Note: The second example can also be written without a comma:

22 February 1945

9 separate figures in numbers of four or more digits:

4,722,526

3,680

Note: There is a modern trend, however, to express figures of five or more digits with spaces instead of commas and figures of four digits with neither a comma nor a space:

4 722 526

3680

10 include a conjunction in a sentence:

He was running very late, *but* he caught the right train.

SEMICOLON

A semicolon is used when a pause is needed that requires more than a comma, but not a full stop. It should only be used occasionally:

1 to separate clauses when a conjunction is not used:

The farm was old and neglected; the barn was falling down; the house was full of rats. (the semicolons replace 'and')

2 when the writer wants the reader to pause longer than with a comma:

Phillip loves cricket; swimming too, but cricket is his passion.

3 to separate items, or to break up a long sentence where some things are already separated with a comma:

The signatures on the letter were those of P Weaver, Professor at the University; M Weaver, doing her Masters Degree; and J Weaver, Principal of the Weaver Institute.

4 to include an adverbial conjunction in a sentence:

John likes playing tennis; however, he loves playing golf!

COLON

A colon is used to:

1 include a quotation:

Do you know the Bible verse: 'For the love of money is the root of all evil'?

2 introduce a list:

There were three excellent students at the Institute: Phillip, Lee and Merryn.

3 make two different statements obvious:

Jane loves sewing and gardening: John loves reading and sleeping.

APOSTROPHE

An apostrophe is used to:

1 show that letters have been removed (contractions): *won't* instead of *will not* and *he's* instead of *he is* or *he has*.

2 explain who owns something:

- One owner – the apostrophe is put before the 's':

Matthew's coat

- More than one owner – the apostrophe is put after the 's':

the girls' bikes

- With some plural nouns the apostrophe goes before the *'s': men's, women's, children's:*

The men's team. The women's craft day. The children's playground.

Note: There are some instances where it is acceptable to use plural nouns without an apostrophe where it is not evident whether the sentence refers to one or many:

Mothers Day, Fathers Day, parents retreat

INVERTED COMMAS (QUOTATION MARKS)

Inverted commas or quotation marks are used to:

1 clearly show a quotation or someone's spoken words:

   Phillip said: 'Do I really have to learn about punctuation?'

2 show the names of books, movies, ships, etc:

   The 'Titanic' was a ship going nowhere.

3 enclose a quotation within a quotation. Use single quotation marks for the outer quotation marks and double quotation marks for the inner quotation:

   Denise said, 'I love that old saying: "A stitch in time saves nine", don't you?'

Note: When ending a sentence with a quotation, close the quotation marks before the full stop.

My favourite quote is: 'Laughter is the best medicine'.

QUESTION MARK

A question mark is used:

1 at the end of a question:

   Who will win the next competition?

2 to show that you are not sure about a date or some other information:

   It happened in June (?) 1960.

EXCLAMATION MARK

An exclamation mark is used to emphasise a feeling or emotion:

1 after interjections:

   Good grief! Oh!

2 after major statements:

   The forest is on fire!

3 after a wish is made:

   I want to win first place!

HYPHEN

A hyphen is used to:

1 join words that go together and would give the wrong meaning if separated:

   self-respect, son-in-law, first-class

2 make the meaning clear:

   seventy-five dollars

3 make the meaning of a word clear when it has the same spelling as another word:

   recount or re-count, recover or re-cover

4 help with pronunciation:

   co-operate, re-employ

BRACKETS (PARENTHESES)

Brackets (parentheses) are used to include information that is not necessary to give meaning to the sentence:

   She quickly got into her car (a red Mercedes) and drove to the police station.

Commas can also be used instead of brackets

   She quickly got into her car, a red Mercedes, and drove to the police station.

DASH

A dash is used to:

1 make a longer pause in the sentence or change direction in the sentence:

   I think I'll travel by train – yes, definitely! (longer pause)

   They won – but only because they cheated! (changing direction)

2 introduce a list (instead of using a colon):

   The best sights in Sydney are – the Opera House, the Harbour Bridge and the Rocks.

Note: However, in modern minimalist editing the colon is the preferred option.

3 make a dramatic statement:

   The Queen came – herself!

CAPITALS

Capitals are very important for:

1 the first word in a sentence and also the first word in a quotation:

   Mike came in and said, 'Let's go to a play!'

2 proper names:

   Michelle, Jaime, Aidan, Cody, Orange, Australia

SOME EXAMPLES OF PUNCTUATED SENTENCES

When he left, the children were very quiet.

People become champion tennis players for three main reasons: they have the talent; they really want to play; and they have the time and money to practise.

Our neighbour, Nina Cooper, is currently in Canberra.

I will not even try: it is too dangerous.

The boys' parents went to see them play at the new oval.

Emma and James moved here on 4 March 2000.

Where are Jane and Richard?

Andrew is David's father-in-law.

We loved the movie; however, we didn't like one of the actors.

Kate is wearing a beautiful dress – made by her mother, Philippa.

Jenny went to South Africa (via Singapore) last week.

Monica asked, 'Where's Charlie?'

'Hey, Charlie!'

CHAPTER 4
MAKING IT WORK AND EDITING IT

How does it work?

How to extend/expand your writing using all parts of speech in:

- present tenses
- past tenses
- future tenses
- all tenses (in a letter)

The rules of editing

Editing

Proofreading

Final Check

HOW DOES IT WORK

EXAMPLE: PRESENT TENSE

Start with a basic piece of writing, in the **present tense**.

> Phillip loves cricket. He is in a team. He plays on Saturdays. He can bat and bowl.

Go to the table of main active verb tenses (page 45) and look at the present tense. Include all the different parts of the present tense in your writing:

> Phillip *loves* cricket. He *is playing* in a team. He *has bowled* and batted. He *has been playing* on Saturdays.

Now include some adjectives:

> Phillip is a *great* guy who loves cricket. He is playing in an *excellent* team. He has bowled and batted. He has been playing on *fine* Saturdays.

Now include some adverbs:

Phillip is a great guy who loves cricket. He is playing *really well* in an excellent team. He has bowled *confidently* and batted *carefully*. He has been playing *enthusiastically* on fine Saturdays.

Now include some conjunctions:

Phillip is a great guy who loves cricket. He is playing really well in an excellent team. He has bowled confidently *and* batted carefully *because* he has had very good coaching. He has been playing enthusiastically on fine Saturdays *since* he started with the team.

Now include some interesting nouns. Maybe a compound noun and a gerund:

Phillip is a great guy who loves cricket. He is playing really well in an excellent team. He has bowled confidently and batted carefully because he has had very good *coaching*. He has been playing enthusiastically on fine Saturdays since he started with the team. Phillip's *cricket bat* and *cricket bag* are his most important *possessions*. Apart from cricket, Phillip loves *swimming*.

Now include some more interesting prepositions:

Phillip is a great guy who loves cricket. He is playing really well in an excellent team. He has bowled confidently and batted carefully because he has had very good coaching. He has been playing enthusiastically on fine Saturdays since he started with the team. They play at Harrison Oval, which is *next to* a beautiful river. They usually have drinks *beneath* the large oak trees. Phillip's cricket bat and cricket bag are his most important possessions. Apart from cricket, Phillip loves swimming.

Now include some more interesting pronouns:

Phillip is a great guy who loves cricket. He is playing really well in an excellent team. He has bowled confidently and batted carefully because he has had very good coaching. *Everyone* thinks he is the best player on the team. Phillip *himself* thinks that there are two players who are better. He has been playing enthusiastically on fine Saturdays since he started with the team. They play at Harrison Oval, which is next to a beautiful river. They usually have drinks beneath the large oak trees. Phillip's cricket bat and cricket bag are his most important possessions. Apart from cricket, Phillip loves swimming.

Now include some dialogue (include an interjection – *Hey!*):

Phillip is a great guy who loves cricket. He is playing really well in an excellent team. He has bowled confidently and batted carefully because he has had very good coaching. Everyone thinks he is the best player on the team. Phillip himself thinks that there are two players who are better. He has been playing enthusiastically on fine Saturdays since he started with the team. They play at Harrison Oval, which is next to a beautiful river. They usually have drinks beneath the large oak trees. Phillip's cricket bat and cricket bag are his most important possessions. Every time the team play well the coach always encourages them by saying: '*Hey! Well done, guys*!' Apart from cricket, Phillip loves swimming.

Now check the punctuation:

Phillip is a great guy who loves cricket. He is playing really well in an excellent team. He has bowled confidently and batted carefully because he has had very good coaching. Everyone thinks he is the best player on the team. Phillip himself thinks that there are two players who are better. He has been playing enthusiastically on fine Saturdays since he started with the team. They play at Harrison Oval, which is next to a beautiful river. They usually have drinks beneath the large oak trees. Phillip's cricket bat and cricket bag are his most important possessions. Every time the team play well the coach always encourages them by saying: 'Hey! Well done, guys!' Apart from cricket, Phillip loves swimming!

Note: This simple procedure is only a guide to help you begin the process of writing. As you develop your own style of expressing your ideas, thoughts and feelings, apply the rules of editing (see page 136).

By referring to the grammatical conventions (parts of speech, tenses, dialogue, punctuation, and so on) and the editing rules, your writing will make sense, be grammatically correct and be interesting for other people to read.

EXAMPLE: PAST TENSE

Here is a basic piece of writing in the *past tense*.

Yong and Acacio went overseas. They flew to Austria. They went to Egypt. They went to London.

Now go to the table of main active verb tenses (page 45) and look at the past tense. Include all the different aspects of the past tense in your writing:

Yong and Acacio *went* overseas. They *were flying* for 21 hours before they *arrived* in Austria. They *had been* in Austria for two days and *took* a flight to Egypt. They *had been travelling* in Egypt for a week when they *flew* to London.

Now include some adjectives:

Yong and Acacio are *good* friends and went overseas. They were flying for 21 hours before they arrived in *beautiful* Austria. They had been in Austria for *two* days and took a flight to *historic* Egypt. They had been travelling in *historic* and *fascinating* Egypt for a week when they flew to London.

Now include some adverbs:

Yong and Acacio are *very* good friends and went overseas *together*. They were flying for *nearly* 21 hours before they arrived in beautiful Austria. They had been in Austria for *almost* two days and took a flight to historic Egypt. They had been travelling in historic and fascinating Egypt for a week when they *finally* flew to London.

Now include some conjunctions:

Yong and Acacio are very good friends and went overseas together *because* they had four weeks off work. They were flying for nearly 21 hours *before* they arrived in beautiful Austria. They had been in Austria for almost two days *before* they took a flight to historic Egypt. They had been travelling in historic and fascinating Egypt for a week *when* they finally flew to London.

Now include some interesting nouns. Maybe a compound noun, an abstract noun and a gerund. As the writing increases in length, it's also a good time to start adding paragraphs to separate the main themes of the writing.

Yong and Acacio are very good friends and went overseas together because they had four weeks off work. They took different types of *luggage*. Acacio took a *suitcase* and Yong took a *backpack*. They were flying for nearly 21 hours before they arrived in *Vienna*, the beautiful *capital* of Austria. They were very glad to be in Vienna as they both decided that *flying* wasn't their favourite *pastime*. There is very little *joy* in *flying*.

They had been in Austria for almost two days before they took a flight to historic Egypt. They spent some time in *Cairo* and saw the *Pyramids of Giza* before travelling down to *Karnak* to see the wonderful temples. They had been travelling in historic and fascinating Egypt for a week when they finally flew to London. They met up with their *friends* and toured all the famous *places* of interest.

Now include some more interesting prepositions:

Yong and Acacio are very good friends and went overseas together *in* June because they had four weeks off work. They took different types of luggage. Acacio took a suit case and Yong took a backpack. They also had some hand luggage that they stowed in the compartment *above* their seats. Yong had a new digital camera that he kept *under* the seat.

They were flying for nearly 21 hours before they arrived in Vienna, the beautiful capital of Austria. They were very glad to be in Vienna as they both decided that flying wasn't their favourite pastime. There is very little joy in flying.

They had been in Austria for almost two days before they took a flight to historic Egypt. They spent some time in Cairo, walking *through* the market place and seeing the Pyramids of Giza before travelling down to Karnak to see the wonderful temples.

They had been travelling in historic and fascinating Egypt for a week, even riding *on* a camel, when they finally flew to London. They met up with their friends and toured all the famous places of interest *around* the city.

Now include some more interesting pronouns:

Acacio and Yong are very good friends and went overseas together in June because they had four weeks off work. They took different types of luggage. Acacio took a suitcase and Yong took a backpack. They also had some hand luggage that they stowed in the compartment above their seats. Yong had bought *himself* a new digital camera that he kept under the seat.

They were flying for nearly 21 hours before they arrived in Vienna, the beautiful capital of Austria. *Everything* in Vienna was clean and lovely. They were very glad to be in Vienna as they both decided that flying wasn't their favourite pastime. There is very little joy in flying.

They had been in Austria for almost two days before they took a flight to historic Egypt. Acacio, *who* spoke Arabic, was an excellent travelling companion in Egypt, because he and Yong were able to tour many places by *themselves*. They spent some time in Cairo, walking through the market places and seeing the Pyramids of Giza before travelling down to Karnak to see the wonderful temples.

They had been travelling in historic and fascinating Egypt for a week, even riding on a camel, when they finally flew to London. They met up with their friends and toured all the famous places of interest around the city.

Now include some dialogue (include an interjection – *Oh!*):

Yong and Acacio are very good friends and went overseas together in June because they had four weeks off work. They took different types of luggage. Acacio took a suitcase and Yong took a backpack. They also had some hand luggage that they stowed in the compartment above their seats. Yong had bought himself a new digital camera that he kept under the seat. They were flying for nearly 21 hours before they arrived in Vienna, the beautiful capital of Austria. Everything in Vienna was clean and lovely. They were very glad to be in Vienna as they both decided that flying wasn't their favourite pastime. At one point, Acacio said, '*Oh! There is very little joy in flying, Yong.*'

They had been in Austria for almost two days before they took a flight to historic Egypt. Acacio, who spoke Arabic, was an excellent travelling companion in Egypt, because he and Yong were able to tour many places by themselves. They spent some time in Cairo, walking through the market places before going to see the Pyramids of Giza. As they were climbing inside one of the pyramids, Yong said to Acacio: '*You know, Kasi, Egypt has one of the richest histories we know.*'

Later they travelled down to Karnak by train to see the wonderful temples. They had been travelling in historic and fascinating Egypt for a week, even riding on a camel, when they finally flew to London. They met up with their friends and toured all the famous places of interest around the city.

Now check the punctuation:

Yong and Acacio are very good friends and went overseas together in June because they had four weeks off work. They took different types of luggage – Acacio took a suitcase and Yong took a backpack. They also had some hand luggage that they stowed in the compartment above their seats. Yong had bought himself a new digital camera that he kept under the seat. They were flying for nearly 21 hours before they arrived in Vienna, the beautiful capital of Austria. Everything in Vienna was clean and lovely. They were very glad to be in Vienna as they both decided that flying wasn't their favourite pastime. At one point, Acacio said: 'Oh! There is very little joy in flying, Yong!'

They had been in Austria for almost two days before they took a flight to historic Egypt. Acacio, who spoke Arabic, was an excellent travelling companion in Egypt, because he and Yong were able to tour many places by themselves. They spent some time in Cairo, walking through the market places before going to see the Pyramids of Giza. As they were climbing inside one of the pyramids, Yong said to Acacio: You know, Kasi, Egypt has one of the richest histories we know!'

Later they travelled down to Karnak by train to see the wonderful temples. They had been travelling in historic and fascinating Egypt for a week, even riding on a camel, when they finally flew to London. They met up with their friends and toured all the famous places of interest around the city.

EXAMPLE: FUTURE TENSE

Here is a basic piece of writing in the *future tense*.

We will go to New Zealand soon. We will fly to Auckland. We will hire a car.

Now go to the Table of Main Active Verb Tenses (page 45) and look at the Future Tense. Then look at the chapter on the Future. Now include all the different aspects of the Future Tense in your writing:

We *are going* to New Zealand. We *leave* in April. We *will fly* to Auckland. We *will be hiring* a car. By the time we get back we *will have seen* some places. We *will have been travelling* for 10 days when we *leave*.

Now include some adjectives:

We are going to the *North* Island of New Zealand. We leave early in April. We will fly to Auckland, the *biggest* city. We will be hiring a *suitable* car. By the time we get back we will have seen some *interesting* and *amazing* places. We will have been travelling for 10 days in that *beautiful* country when we leave.

Now include some adverbs:

We are going to the North Island of New Zealand. We leave *really* early in April. We will fly to Auckland, the biggest city. We will be hiring a suitable car. By the time we get back we will have seen some interesting and *absolutely* amazing places. We will have been travelling for 10 days in that *truly* beautiful country when we leave.

Now include some conjunctions:

We are going to the North Island of New Zealand. We leave really early in April *and* we will fly to Auckland, the biggest city *where* we will be hiring a suitable car. By the time we get back we will have seen some absolutely great and amazing places *because* we intend to see the beautiful scenery *and* experience some of the Maori culture. I have been told about the Maori culture *since* I was a child *and* some relatives came to visit us. We will have been travelling for 10 days in that truly beautiful country when we leave.

Now include some interesting nouns. Maybe some compound nouns and gerunds:

We are going to the North Island of New Zealand where we will enjoy some *driving*, *sailing* and *sightseeing*. We leave really early in April and we will fly to Auckland, the biggest city where we will be hiring a suitable car. I'm not that happy about *flying* though. By the time we get back we will have seen some absolutely great and amazing places because we intend to see the beautiful scenery and experience some of the Maori culture. I have been told about the Maori culture since I was a child and some relatives came to visit us.

Our two favourite places to visit will be the *Bay of Islands* and *Rotorua*. We will buy some *souvenirs* for the family, so I hope our *suitcases* will not be too overloaded. I always buy a *tea towel* when we go somewhere new. We will have been travelling for 10 days in that truly beautiful country when we leave.

Now include some more interesting prepositions:

We are going to the North Island of New Zealand where we will enjoy some driving, sailing and sightseeing. We leave really early in April and we will fly to Auckland, the biggest city where we will be hiring a suitable car and travel *around* the country. I'm not that happy about flying though. By the time we get back we will have seen some absolutely great and amazing places because we intend to see the beautiful scenery and experience some of the Maori culture. I have been told about the Maori culture since I was a child and some relatives came to visit us.

Our two favourite places to visit will be the Bay of Islands and Rotorua. We can't wait to board a boat and sail *around* the Bay of Islands and go *through* the famous Hole-in-the-Rock. Then we plan to soak up all the Maori culture. We will visit the Waitangi Treaty House and see the famous ceremonial canoe *nearby*. At Rotorua we will visit a Maori village and watch the children dive *from* the bridge. We will be *among* the people who do the famous Haka and we'll enjoy the poi dancing. We can't wait to see the geysers shoot *into* the air.

We will buy some souvenirs for the family, so I hope our suitcases will not be too overloaded. I always buy a tea towel when we go somewhere new. We will have been travelling for 10 days in that truly beautiful country when we leave.

Now include some more interesting pronouns:

We are going to the North Island of New Zealand where we will enjoy some driving, sailing and sightseeing. We leave really early in April and we will fly to Auckland, the biggest city where we will be hiring a suitable car and travel around the country *ourselves*. I'm not that happy about flying though. By the time we get back we will have seen some absolutely great and amazing places because we intend to see the beautiful scenery and experience some of the Maori culture. I have been told about the Maori culture since I was a child and some relatives came to visit us.

Our two favourite places to visit will be the Bay of Islands and Rotorua. We can't wait to board a boat and sail around the Bay of Islands and go through the famous Hole-in-the-Rock. Then we plan to soak up all the Maori culture. We will visit the Waitangi Treaty House and see the famous ceremonial canoe nearby. At Rotorua we will visit a Maori village and watch the children dive from the bridge. We will be among the people who do the famous Haka and we'll enjoy the poi dancing. *Everyone* enjoys watching the All Blacks do the Haka. We can't wait to see the geysers shoot into the air.

We will buy some souvenirs for the family, so I hope our suitcases will not be too overloaded. I always buy a tea towel when we go somewhere new. We will have been travelling for 10 days in that truly beautiful country when we leave.

Now include some dialogue: (include an interjection – *hey*!)

We are going to the North Island of New Zealand where we will enjoy some driving, sailing and sightseeing. We leave really early in April and we will fly to Auckland, the biggest city where we will be hiring a suitable car and travel around the country ourselves. I'm not that happy about flying though. By the time we get back we will have seen some absolutely great and amazing places because we intend to see the beautiful scenery and experience some of the Maori culture. I have been told about the Maori culture since I was a child and some relatives came to visit us.

Our two favourite places to visit will be the Bay of Islands and Rotorua. We can't wait to board a boat and sail around the Bay of Islands and go through the famous Hole-in-the-Rock. Then we plan to soak up all the Maori culture. We will visit the Waitangi Treaty House and see the famous ceremonial canoe nearby. At Rotorua we will visit a Maori village and watch the children dive from the bridge.

We will be among the people who do the famous Haka and we'll enjoy the poi dancing. Everyone enjoys watching the All Blacks do the Haka. Most people who watch the All Blacks say: "*Hey, don't be late or you'll miss the Haka*!" We can't wait to see the geysers shoot into the air.

We will buy some souvenirs for the family, so I hope our suitcases will not be too overloaded. I always buy a tea towel when we go somewhere new. We will have been travelling for 10 days in that truly beautiful country when we leave.

Now check the punctuation:

We are going to the North Island of New Zealand where we will enjoy some driving, sailing and sightseeing. We leave really early in April and we will fly to Auckland, the biggest city where we will be hiring a suitable car and travel around the country ourselves. I'm not that happy about flying though.

By the time we get back we will have seen some absolutely great and amazing places because we intend to see the beautiful scenery and experience some of the Maori culture. I have been told about the Maori culture since I was a child and some relatives came to visit us.

Our two favourite places to visit will be the Bay of Islands and Rotorua. We can't wait to board a boat and sail around the Bay of Islands and go through the famous Hole-in-the-Rock. Then we plan to soak up all the Maori culture. We will visit the Waitangi Treaty House and see the famous ceremonial canoe nearby.

At Rotorua we will visit a Maori village and watch the children dive from the bridge. We will be among the people who do the famous Haka and we'll enjoy the poi dancing. Everyone enjoys watching the All Blacks do the Haka. Most people who watch the All Blacks say: "Hey, don't be late or you'll miss the Haka!"

We can't wait to see the geysers shoot into the air. We will buy some souvenirs for the family, so I hope our suitcases will not be too overloaded. I always buy a tea towel when we go somewhere new. We will have been travelling for 10 days in that truly beautiful country when we leave.

Note: These simple procedures are only a guide to help you begin the process of writing. As you develop your own style of expressing your ideas, thoughts and feelings, apply the rules of editing.

By referring to the grammatical conventions (parts of speech, tenses, dialogue, punctuation and so on) and the editing rules, your writing will make sense, be grammatically correct and be interesting for other people to read.

A BASIC LETTER SHOWING ALL VERB TENSES

Start with the present tenses:

How *are* you? I hope you *are enjoying* your holiday. You *have been* away for a long time. We know you *have been travelling*.

Now include the past tenses:

How are you? I hope you are enjoying your holiday. You have been away for a long time. We know you have been travelling. We *went* to the tennis last weekend. They *were playing* at the Tennis Centre. We *had bought* the tickets weeks ago. The players *had been competing* all week.

Now include the future tenses:

How are you? I hope you are enjoying your holiday. You have been away for a long time. We know you have been travelling. We went to the tennis last weekend. They were playing at the Tennis Centre. We had bought the tickets weeks ago. The players had been competing all week. We *will travel* to Sydney next week. We *will be going* to a wine tasting. *Will* you *have been* to Rome by then? You*'ll have been travelling* for six weeks.

Now include some conditional tenses:

How are you? I hope you are enjoying your holiday. You have been away for a long time. We know you have been travelling. We went to the tennis last weekend. They were playing at the Tennis Centre. We had bought the tickets weeks ago. The players had been competing all week. We will travel to Sydney next week. We will be going to a wine tasting. Will you have been to Rome by then? You'll have been travelling for six weeks. We're glad you had a lift to the airport. Andre thought he *would take* you if you needed him. He *would've been waiting* with you if you had wanted company. He *will* pick you up if you like.

Now include some adverbs:

How are you? I hope you are *really* enjoying your holiday. You have been away for a *very* long time. We know you have been travelling and hope to arrive in Rome *tomorrow*. We went to the tennis last weekend. They were playing at the Tennis Centre. We had bought the tickets weeks ago. The players had been competing all week, *very enthusiastically*. We will travel to Sydney *again* next week. We will be going to a wine tasting. Will you have been to Rome by then? You'll have been travelling for six weeks. We're glad you had a lift to the airport. Andre thought he would take you if you needed him. He would've been waiting with you if you had wanted company. He will *happily* pick you up if you like.

Now include some conjunctions:

How are you? I hope you are really enjoying your holiday, *because* you deserve it. You have been away for a very long time. We know you have been travelling and hope to arrive in Rome tomorrow. We went to the tennis last weekend. They were playing at the Tennis Centre. We had bought the tickets weeks ago. The players had been competing all week, very enthusiastically. We will travel to Sydney again next week, *as* we will be going to a wine tasting. I can't drink wine; *nevertheless*, I'm going to enjoy the trip. Will you have been to Rome by then? You'll have been travelling for six weeks. We're glad you had a lift to the airport. Andre thought he would take you if you needed him *and* he would've been waiting with you if you had wanted company. He will happily pick you up if you like.

Now include some more interesting nouns:

How are you, my *friend*? I hope you are really enjoying your holiday, because you deserve it. You have been away for a very long time. We know you have been travelling and hope to arrive in Rome tomorrow. Are you using *money* or your *credit cards*? *Travelling* is very expensive isn't it?

We went to the tennis last weekend. It was the *Final*! They were playing at the Tennis Centre. We had bought the tickets weeks ago. The players had been competing all week, very enthusiastically. We took our *camera* and the *binoculars*. The *tennis* and the *action* were great. The *champion* won. The *crowd* went wild!

We will travel to Sydney again next week, then on to the *Hunter Valley*, as we will be going to a wine tasting. I can't drink wine; nevertheless, I'm going to enjoy the trip.

Will you have been to Rome by then? You'll have been travelling for six weeks. Don't forget to see the *Colosseum* and the *Vatican City*.

We're glad you had a lift to the airport. Andre thought he would take you if you needed him and he would've been waiting with you if you had wanted company. It's not much *fun* waiting there. He will happily pick you up from the *airport* if you like.

Now include some adjectives:

How are you, my *dear* friend? I hope you are really enjoying your *fabulous* holiday, because you deserve it. You have been away for a very long time. We know you have been travelling and hope to arrive in Rome tomorrow. Are you using money or your credit cards? Travelling is very expensive isn't it?

We went to the tennis last weekend. It was the Final! They were playing at the Tennis Centre. We had bought the tickets weeks ago. The *fantastic* players had been competing all week, very enthusiastically. We took our camera and the binoculars. The tennis and the action were great. The champion won. The crowd went wild!

We will travel to Sydney again next week, then on to the Hunter Valley, as we will be going to an *exclusive* wine tasting. I can't drink wine; nevertheless, I'm going to enjoy the trip.

Will you have been to *historic* Rome by then? You'll have been travelling for six weeks. Don't forget to see the Colosseum and the Vatican City.

We're glad you had a lift to the *international* airport. Andre thought he would take you if you needed him and he would've been waiting with you if you had wanted company. It's not much fun waiting there. He will happily pick you up from the *new* airport if you like.

Now include some more interesting prepositions:

How are you, my dear friend? I hope you are really enjoying your fabulous holiday, because you deserve it. You have been away for a very long time. We know you have been travelling *around* Europe and hope to arrive in Rome tomorrow. Are you using money or your credit cards? Travelling is very expensive isn't it?

We went to the tennis last weekend. It was the Final! They were playing at the Tennis Centre. We were *in* the Centre Court, *next* to the main Stadium. We had bought the tickets weeks ago. The fantastic players had been competing all week, very enthusiastically. We took our camera and the binoculars. Two of my favourite players were in the commentary box *above* us. The tennis and the action were great. The champion won. The crowd went wild!

We will travel to Sydney again next week, then on to the Hunter Valley, as we will be going to an exclusive wine tasting. We will be *among* some of the best vineyards in the country. I can't drink wine; nevertheless, I'm going to enjoy the trip.

Will you have been to historic Rome by then? You'll have been travelling for six weeks. Don't forget to see the Colosseum and the Vatican City. The Roman Forum is *near* your hotel too.

We're glad you had a lift to the international airport. Andre thought he would take you if you needed him and he would've been waiting with you if you had wanted company. It's not much fun waiting there *next to* the nervous passengers. He will happily pick you up from the new airport if you like.

Now include some more interesting pronouns:

How are you, my dear friend? I hope you are really enjoying your fabulous holiday, because you deserve it. You have been away for a very long time. We know you have been travelling around Europe and hope to arrive in Rome tomorrow. Are you using money or your credit cards? Travelling is very expensive isn't it? *Everything* seems to cost more overseas.

We went to the tennis last weekend. It was the Final! They were playing at the Tennis Centre. We were in the Centre Court, next to the Stadium. We had bought the tickets weeks ago. The fantastic players had been competing all week, very enthusiastically. We took our camera and the binoculars. Two of my favourite players, *who* were champions in their time, were in the commentary box above us. The tennis and the action were great. The champion won. The crowd went wild! *Everybody* enjoyed the match!

We will travel to Sydney again next week, then on to the Hunter Valley, as we will be going to an exclusive wine tasting. We will be among some of the best vineyards in the country. I can't drink wine; nevertheless, I'm going to enjoy the trip.

Will you have been to historic Rome by then? You'll have been travelling for six weeks. Don't forget to see the Colosseum and the Vatican City. You may even see the Pope *himself*. The Roman Forum is near your hotel too.

We're glad you had a lift to the international airport. Andre thought he would take you *himself* if you needed him and he would've been waiting with you if you had wanted company. It's not much fun waiting there next to the nervous passengers. He will happily pick you up from the new airport if you like.

Now include some dialogue (include an interjection – Hey!):

How are you, my dear friend? I hope you are really enjoying your fabulous holiday, because you deserve it. You have been away for a very long time. We know you have been travelling around Europe and hope to arrive in Rome tomorrow. Are you using money or your credit cards? Travelling is very expensive isn't it? Everything seems to cost more overseas. The family has a message for you:

'Hey, guys! Have a great time! Wish we were there! Love you!'

We went to the tennis last weekend. It was the Final! They were playing at the Tennis Centre. We were in the Centre Court, next to the Stadium. We had bought the tickets weeks ago. The fantastic players had been competing all week, very enthusiastically. We took our camera and the binoculars. Two of my favourite players, who were champions in their time, were in the commentary box above us. The tennis and the action were great. The champion won. The crowd went wild! Everybody enjoyed the match!

We will travel to Sydney again next week, then on to the Hunter Valley, as we will be going to an exclusive wine tasting. We will be among some of the best vineyards in the country. I can't drink wine; nevertheless, I'm going to enjoy the trip.

Will you have been to historic Rome by then? You'll have been travelling for six weeks. Don't forget to see the Colosseum and the Vatican City. You may even see the Pope himself. The Roman Forum is near your hotel too.

We're glad you had a lift to the international airport. Andre thought he would take you himself if you needed him and he would've been waiting with you if you had wanted company. It's not much fun waiting there next to the nervous passengers. He will happily pick you up from the new airport if you like.

Now check the punctuation.

Note: This simple procedure is only a guide to help you begin the process of writing. As you develop your own style of expressing your ideas, thoughts and feelings, apply the rules of editing.

By referring to the grammatical conventions (parts of speech, tenses, dialogue, punctuation, and so on.) and the editing rules, your writing will make sense, be grammatically correct and be interesting for other people to read.

THE RULES OF EDITING

Now that you've put what you've learned into practice, it's time to review and check your written work. The following is a useful checklist for checking your work.

EDITING

- Have you used a variety of the parts of speech? (see Chapter 1 Parts of Speech: at a glance).
- Have you used the correct verb tenses? (see the table of main active verb tenses or conditional tenses or passive verb forms)
- Are there any other ways of expressing important or dramatic points?
- Are your sentences complete?
- Check the punctuation.
- Have you included dialogue in your narrative?
- Read it through. Does it make sense? Would it make sense to somebody else?
- Do you need to rewrite any part of your work?

PROOFREADING

- With your final draft it's a good idea to check a printed copy rather than from the computer screen.
- Use a dictionary to check your spelling.
- Remember that a spell-check on a computer can only pick up a word spelt incorrectly – it cannot pick up a wrong word that is spelt correctly!
- Have you used the correct written language form (essay, report, narrative, poem, etc)?
- Have you included all the main points?
- Are the main points in order of importance or date?
- Have you used a new paragraph for each main point?
- Have you included an introduction and a conclusion (where applicable)?
- Are the main points included in the introduction and the conclusion?
- Have you included references (where applicable)?
- Have you included a reference list or bibliography (where applicable)?

FINAL CHECKS

- Ask somebody else to read your work and give you some feedback.
- Have you included any other necessary parts – such as the title, the date, your name?
- Have you made sure that any corrections on a computer have printed out correctly?

CHAPTER 5
MAJOR FORMS OF WRITTEN LANGUAGE

Narrative

Recount

Procedure

Explanation

Exposition

Response

Report
General report
Research lab report
Fieldwork report
Research proposal (case study)

Essay
General explanation
Descriptive essay
Narrative essay
Discursive essay
Expository essay
Analytical essay
Argumentative essay

NARRATIVE

Narratives are used for creative writing and include novels, short stories, fairy tales, fables, plays, some poems and words for songs, films, TV programs and so on. They can also be used to write historical biographies. Generally narratives are written to entertain the reader. They are usually written in a set format. There are two main formats:

1 **Introduction**

    setting

    theme

    characters

    plot

Development

    complications/problems

    dialogue

Conclusion

    how the problem is solved

2 **Orientation**

    who? what? where? when?

Complication

    the problem

    what goes wrong?

Resolution

    how the problem is solved

    things go back to normal – but something (such as the situation, or the characters) is now different.

Coda

    (optional) shows how the main character/s has changed and what has been learned from the experience.

All parts of speech are used, especially descriptive language, including figures of speech – such as metaphors and similes. Past tense is generally used and dialogue is an important component of a narrative.

RECOUNT

Recounts re-tell events. They can include autobiographies, biographies, short stories, newspaper reports, letters, journals, diaries, some poems, historical events, films, television documentaries and records. The events are usually written down in chronological order. They often use a set format.

    Explanation

    Events in chronological order

    Evaluation

All parts of speech are used. Descriptive language is important and so are time words and action verbs. Recounts are written in the past tense.

PROCEDURE

Procedures are used to explain the way to do something using facts. For example they include recipes, experiments and map-reading instructions. They are often written in a set format.

- The reason for the procedure – the goal
- The materials needed
- The method

All parts of speech can be included. Phrases are often used instead of whole sentences. Procedures usually begin with a verb in the present simple tense as a command.

- <u>Break</u> the eggs into a bowl
- <u>Mix</u> the following substances
- <u>Look</u> at the map

EXPLANATION

Explanations are used to show how and why things occur – phenomena. These can include seasons, rainfall, tides, reproduction, storms and meteors, for example. Explanations are found in scientific textbooks, films, television reports and online. They are usually written in a set format.

- Introduce the phenomena
- Explain the phenomena in order to show cause and effect

There are generally no people involved in explanations. Definitions are important. Scientific and technical words are used and are often in phrases instead of sentences. All parts of speech can be used, especially conjunctions, with present simple verb tense. The active verb form is generally used, but sometimes the passive is more effective.

- The moon *influences* the tides. (active)
- Tides *are influenced* by the moon. (passive)

You must acknowledge the source of any information you have researched. If you do not know how to do this, check with your university, school, public library or online.

EXPOSITION

Expositions are used to argue a topic or persuade the reader about a subject or an issue from a particular point of view. Subjects can include all manner of things, such as violence, television, crime and smoking. Expositions are found in information books and booklets, newspapers, letters to the editor, editorials and so on. They are written in a set format.

The proposition to be maintained or proved: the thesis

The argument

Conclusion – reinforcing the argument

All parts of speech can be used, especially conjunctions – *however, therefore, because, nevertheless;* adverbs – *particularly, usually, possibly, finally;* modal verbs – *must, should, mustn't, shouldn't,* for example:

Lollies <u>shouldn't</u> be eaten in school.

The passive verb form is often included:

When lollies <u>are eaten</u> by children in school . . .

RESPONSE

Responses are used to discuss an artistic piece, such as a musical performance, a painting, a sculpture, a play, or a film. Responses can be found in newspapers in the form of reviews. They are usually written in a set way.

- Title, author, etc.
- Explanation of work and where it is/was
- Description of work
- Judgement on work
    - evaluation
    - negative or positive response to the work

All parts of speech can be used, especially descriptive words. Present tense is the most appropriate, but past tense can be used as well.

REPORT

GENERAL REPORT

General reports provide and explain information. They can be found in scientific publications, films, television programs and online. If a general report is to be written, it is usually about a particular topic. The topic is often provided by a lecturer, a teacher or an examiner and the student is given time to research the topic. A general report is usually set out as follows:

- introduction with general comments
- description in more detail
- summary
- reference list/bibliography
- appendices (see Glossary).

Reports are divided into separate parts, using headings, dot points or numbers. All parts of speech can be used. General reports are usually written in the present tense:

> Medical research has found . . .

and in the third person (*he/she/it/they*). Reports may require technical vocabulary. Charts, diagrams and illustrations are often required in a report. A reference list or a bibliography must be included at the end of a report.

You must acknowledge the source of any information you have researched. If you do not know how to do this, check with your university, school, public library or online.

RESEARCH LAB REPORT

Many science-based subjects require you to write lab reports, which include the following features:

- abstract
- introduction
- methods (including procedures)
- results
- discussion
- reference list (where applicable)
- appendices where applicable (see Glossary).

Lab reports are generally written in past tense, using technical language. Some parts of the report may be written in present tense or even future tense, especially in the abstract, introduction and discussion. All parts of speech may be used.

FIELDWORK REPORT

Some courses such as physical and environmental sciences require some fieldwork with a report. These reports are usually structured in the following way:

- title
- introduction with the aim of the report
- methods
- presentation of data
- discussion
- conclusion
- reference list/bibliography (where applicable)
- appendices where applicable (see Glossary).

All parts of speech may be used. Technical language is a necessary part of this type of report. Past tense is generally used with some use of present tense and future tense in the introduction and conclusion.

RESEARCH PROPOSAL (CASE STUDY)

Courses that include Sociology, Social Administration and Social Policy may require a research proposal or case study. These might be structured in the following way:

- title
- abstract
- aims and objectives
- time span; items that may need to be considered include:
    - further planning and approval
    - ethical approval
    - pre-tests or pilots
    - collection of data
    - analysis/synthesis of data
    - writing-up
    - dissemination of information, participation in policy formation, etc.
- background
- research design
- methodology
- significance
- budget
- reference list

All parts of speech may be used. Technical language is necessary in this type of report. All verb tenses might be used.

ESSAY

Essays are writing forms that are used to describe something, discuss something, express a point of view or persuade the reader on any topic. The topic is usually given by a lecturer, a teacher or an examiner. There is often a set length for an essay. You are expected to discuss the topic in a set format.

- title
- introduction
- the development of your essay in the main body
- conclusion
- reference list/bibliography (where applicable)
- appendices where applicable (see Glossary).

There are no headings or dot points used in an essay. Each paragraph should discuss a different point, mentioned briefly in your introduction. The points should be in logical or chronological order. All parts of speech can be used. Logical and objective language should be used. An essay is usually written in present tense. However, if your essay is about an historical event, then past tense would be used. Some essays, especially science fiction, may be written in the future tense. If you are given time to research your essay, you will need to include references in the essay and a reference list/bibliography at the end.

You must acknowledge the source of any information you have researched. If you don't know how to do this, check with your university, school, public library or online.

DESCRIPTIVE ESSAY

Descriptive essays are used to describe something. For example:

'A Beach Holiday Resort'

All parts of speech can be used, especially descriptive language. Present tense would be most common for descriptive essays:

'The Resort at Stoney Island is the best place in the world!'

NARRATIVE ESSAY

Narrative essays tell a story.

'My Trip to the Snow'

'The Story of My Life'

These essays are mainly written in chronological order. There should be a beginning and an end to the story. They can take the form of an autobiography or a biography. All parts of speech can be used. Past tense would be most common for a narrative essay.

DISCURSIVE ESSAY

Discursive essays are used to look at a topic from different points of view – for and against. For example:

'Smoking in Public Places'

Discussion is the main element of these essays. You must investigate the topic from various points of view – fairly and without strong, personal opinions.

All parts of speech can be used, especially conjunctions. Use modal verbs – *should, could, would*, and so on. Present tense would be used.

EXPOSITORY ESSAY

Expository essays are used to explain something, for example:

'How to Use a Computer'

All parts of speech can be used. Present simple tense is mainly used.

ANALYTICAL ESSAY

Analytical essays separate the topic into parts to examine or explain it further. For example:

'Analyse the Problem of Pollution in Large Cities'

All parts of speech can be used, especially conjunctions. Present tense would be most common. Use modal verbs – *should, ought to, must*, and so on.

ARGUMENTATIVE ESSAY

Argumentative essays attempt to persuade the reader to a particular point of view, for example:

'Stricter Censorship for Films and TV'

You would be expected to discuss both sides of the argument, comparing and contrasting them. Give explanations where necessary. Reasoned arguments should lead to a logical conclusion – your opinion. All parts of speech can be used, especially conjunctions. Modal verbs – *must, should, ought to, would, shouldn't, must not*, and so on. Present tense would be most common.

GLOSSARY

ADVERBIAL

An adverb, adverbial phrase or a preposition phrase used to explain the time, manner or place of the action described in a sentence.

> Jade played *yesterday*. (adverb)
>
> She played *like a professional*. (adverbial phrase)
>
> She played *in the band*. (preposition phrase)

APPENDIX

Appendix (singular), appendices or appendixes (plural). An appendix contains extra material to be used, but not in the text of the essay, report, book or document. The material supports claims made in the body of the text, but is usually too long to be included in the text itself.

ASPECT

A verbal category or form expressing inception (beginning), duration or completion.

> *simple, continuous, perfect, perfect continuous*

CLAUSE

A sentence, which is part of a larger sentence, is called a clause. A clause must have a Subject and a Predicate. A clause that can stand alone as a sentence is called the independent clause or the main clause. A clause which cannot stand alone is called the dependent clause or the subordinate clause.

> *John and I went to Fiji* **and** *John played golf at a resort*. (2 independent clauses)
>
> *John and I went to Fiji* **because** *we wanted a holiday*. (1 independent clause & 1 dependent clause)

COMPLEMENT

Some **Transitive verbs** need more than an Object to make the Predicate complete. The word or words that complete the Predicate of a sentence = the Complement.

She *found* (verb) *the man* (object) *asleep* (complement).

Some **Intransitive verbs** do not require an Object, but may need a Complement to complete the Predicate of a sentence.

Birds *sing* (verb) *beautifully* (complement).

DETERMINER

A Determiner is used before a noun. It limits a noun. The principal determiners are the articles. Other Determines include some adjectives and pronouns.

The book was in *a* cupboard. (articles)

Look at *my* photo. (possessive adjective)

This is my favourite book. (demonstrative pronoun)

GERUND

A gerund is a verb form with *–ing* on the end. It looks like the present participle, but always acts as a noun.

Reading and *gardening* give me great pleasure.

GRAMMAR

The rules of a language to show the relationship between words; and how to put words, phrases and clauses together to form sentences. These rules include basic sounds and pronunciation.

INFINITIVE

The infinitive names a verb without referring to the doer of the action, the number or the tense of the verb. The preposition *to* before the infinitive is not always used.

The children went *to play* with their friends. (the infinitive with *to*)

We decided *to go* and *buy* a car. (the infinitive with and without *to*)

MODIFIER

A modifier is a word, phrase or clause that changes, restricts or qualifies the meaning of another word or group of words in a sentence.

Adverbs can modify:

    verbs   He walks *slowly*.

    adjectives   She is a *very* pretty girl.

    adverbs   The wind blew *quite* suddenly.

Adjectives can modify nouns.

    She was given a *sour* apple.

Adjectives can modify pronouns.

    She wanted *another* one.

Nouns can modify other nouns.

    Nate runs a *ballet* school.

Preposition phrases can modify nouns.

    He wanted a bottle *of water*.

Adjective clauses can modify nouns.

    The baby *who was hungry* cried.

MODIFY

To change, restrict or qualify the meaning of a word or group of words.

OBJECT

A noun or its equivalent governed by an active transitive verb or by a preposition.

    The *direct object* to a verb: She made *some* cakes.

    The *indirect object* to a verb: She made *the* children some cakes.

    The *object* of a preposition: The forest was destroyed *by* fire.

PARTICIPLE

A word formed from verbs and used: (a) with auxiliaries to form tenses or (b) as adjectives.

    is *going*   (present participle to form present continuous tense)

    has *gone*   (past participle to form present perfect tense)

    working man (adjective using a present participle)

PHRASAL VERB

A verb followed by a particle (adverb or preposition) that gives a different meaning from the verb alone. Phrasal verbs are used in spoken English and informal texts.

    The plane *took off*. (verb + adverb)

    I can't *put up with* the noise any longer. (verb + adverb + preposition)

PHRASE

A combination of words that do not make complete sense: *in the water; through rain and snow; quite slowly; as well as*

PREDICATE

The word or words in a sentence, which say something about the person or thing denoted by the Subject. The predicate consists of a verb in a sentence or clause - together with its object/s, complements, adverbials (adjuncts) and modifiers, etc.

    Rosie *found* (verb) *her brother* (object) *sleeping* (complement) *in the cot* (adverbial).

QUALIFIER

A qualifier is a word, phrase or clause that describes another word and gives quality to it. It can also limit or specify another word and make it less general. A qualifier is also thought of as another word for a modifier.

Adjectives can qualify <u>nouns</u>.

    She is an *exquisite* <u>ballerina</u>.

Adverbs can qualify <u>verbs</u>.

    She <u>danced</u> *quite superbly*.

Articles (the) can qualify <u>nouns</u>.

    She won *the* <u>scholarship</u>.

Preposition phrases can qualify <u>verbs</u>.

    She <u>danced</u> *around the room*.

Adjective clauses can qualify <u>nouns</u>.

    The girl *who danced* was her <u>daughter</u>.

QUALIFY

To describe or attribute a quality to another word, especially a noun. To specify a word or phrase. To limit or modify the meaning of another word.

SENTENCE

A group of words that make complete sense - containing or implying a Subject and a Predicate - and convey a statement, a question, a command or an exclamation.

    Mary (subject) *loves Sam* (predicate). (statement)

    Go home! (predicate) (command - *You* is implied.)

    Who (subject) *broke the window?* (predicate) (question)

    They (subject) *won the cup!* (predicate) (exclamation)

SUBJECT

The word or words of a sentence (mainly a noun or pronoun) denoting the person or thing, about which something is stated or asked in the Predicate.

    May is having a sleep. (subject in a statement - noun)

    Who is having a sleep? (subject in a question - pronoun)

VERBALS

A verb form, which is used as another part of speech. There are three types of verbals - *infinitives, gerunds, participles*.

    To love is wonderful. (The Infinitive used as a noun)

    Swimming is a great sport. (Gerunds are nouns)

    She is a *working* woman. (Present participle as an adjective)

    The *burnt* toast was dreadful. (Past participle as an adjective)

INDEX

A

a (indefinite article) 5, 30-33

abbreviations 117

abstract nouns 12, 13, 126

active verbs 44, 45, 46-58, 104

   converting to passive 69-71

adjective (relative) clauses 18, 21, 23-24, 107

adjective phrases 23, 103

adjectives 5, 22-29, 123, 125, 128, 133

   comparative 23

   definition of 5, 22

   demonstrative 23

   descriptive 23, 26-28

   distributive 23

   ending in -ing or –ed 25

   examples of 27-29

   forming adverbs 92-93

   interrogative 23

   nouns as 5, 22

   order for more than one 26-28

   possessive 16, 23, 116

   quantitative 23

   superlative 23

   types of 23

   use of 5, 22

   verbs that go with 22

   see also participles

adverb clauses 93, 104-105, 108

adverb phrases 93, 103

adverbial conjunctions 95, 96, 98, 102

adverbs 7, 89-95, 124, 126, 128-129, 132

   definition of 7, 89

   degree 89, 92

   ending in –ly 92-93

   examples of 94

   formed from adjectives 92-93, 94

   frequency 89, 92

   interrogative 90

   manner 89, 91, 92

   and phrasal verbs 44, 106

   place 89, 92, 93, 95

   position of 91, 93

   reason 90, 93

   relative 24, 90, 107

   sentence 89, 92

   substitute 90

   time 89, 92, 93, 95

   types of 89-90

use of 7, 89

an (indefinite article) 5, 30, 31, 32, 33

apostrophes 119

appendix, definition of – see Glossary

articles 5, 30-33

   definite 5, 30, 31, 33

   definition of 5, 30

   examples using 33

   indefinite 5, 31-32, 33

   use of 5, 30

auxiliary verbs 40-41, 62-68, 77, 81, 85, 109-110, 114-116

   contractions 41, 114-116

   forming tenses 40-41, 44-45

   modal 40-41, 62-68, 70, 109, 110, 114-116

   plain 40-41, 77, 81, 85, 109-110, 114-116

   in questions 109-111

B

brackets 121

C

capital letters 122

clauses 106-108

   adjective (relative) 18, 21, 23-24, 104, 107, 108

   adverb 93, 105, 108

   conjunction 97, 108

   connective adjective 18, 21, 24, 107

   defining adjective 18, 21, 24, 107

   definition of 106

   dependent 13, 23, 93, 102, 106-108

   independent 96, 101-102, 106

   non-defining adjective 18, 21, 24, 107

   noun 13, 108

   pronoun 21

   relative (adjective) 18, 21, 23-24, 104, 107, 108

   types of 107-108

collective nouns 12, 13

   place of apostrophe 119

colons 119

commas 117-118

common nouns 11, 13

comparative adjectives 23

complement of sentence 101

complex sentences 102

compound nouns 12, 13, 124, 126, 129

compound sentences 102

conditional tenses 44, 59-61, 132

   perfect 44, 59, 60, 61, 69

   perfect continuous 44, 59, 61

   present 44, 59, 60, 61

   present continuous 44, 60, 61

   zero 59-61

conjunction clause 97, 108

conjunction phrases 97, 103

conjunctions 8, 96-98, 124, 126, 129, 132-133

   adverbial 96, 98, 102

   coordinating 96, 97, 102

definition of 8, 96

examples 97-98

subordinating 96, 97-98, 102, 108

use of 8, 96, 102

connective adjective (relative) clauses 18, 21, 24, 107

connectors *see* conjunctions 8, 96

contractions 41, 45, 49, 51, 114-116

negatives 115-116

coordinating conjunctions 96, 97, 102

count nouns 11, 13

indefinite article before 32, 33

D

dashes 121

defining adjective (relative) clauses 18, 21, 24, 107

definite article 5, 30, 31, 33

demonstrative adjectives 23

demonstrative pronouns 19

dependent clauses 13, 23, 93, 102, 106-108

descriptive adjectives 23, 26-28

determiners 6, 16, 23, 30

dialogue 124-125, 127, 130, 135

contractions 116

interjections 8, 99, 124-125, 127, 130, 135

modal verbs 68

pronouns 15, 16

questions 111

direct object 39

direct speech 112-113

distributive adjectives 23

E

editing, rules of 136

emphatic pronouns 16-17

essays, format and features of 143-144

analytical 144

argumentative 144

descriptive 143

discursive 144

expository 144

narrative 143-144

exclamation marks 8, 99, 120

explanations, format and features of 139

expositions, format and features of 140

F

fieldwork reports, features of 142

full stops 117

future tense 44, 45, 57-58, 128

continuous 44, 45, 57, 80, 84, 88

examples 58

other ways of expressing 58

perfect 44, 45, 57, 80, 84, 88

perfect continuous 44, 45, 57, 80, 84, 88

simple 44, 45, 57, 69, 80, 84, 88

see also irregular verbs

G

generalising a noun 5, 30-32

gerunds 12, 13, 43, 124, 126, 129

H

hyphens 121

I

imperative mood 42

indefinite article 5, 31-32, 33

indefinite pronouns 20

independent clauses 96, 101-102, 106

indicative mood 42

indirect object 39

indirect speech 112-113

infinitives 42-43, 70, 73-76

    split 43

interjection phrases 99, 103

interjections 8, 99, 124-125, 127, 130, 135

    definition of 8, 99

    types of 99

    use of 8, 99

interrogative adjectives 23

interrogative pronouns 19

intransitive verbs 39

inverted commas 120

irregular verbs 38, 72

    list of 73-76

    for present simple tense 72

    to be 77-80

    to have 81-84

    to do 85-88

L

linking words *see* conjunctions

M

mass nouns 11, 13, 31

modal (auxiliary) verbs 40, 62-68, 70, 109-110, 114-116

    in dialogue 68

    for questions 109-110

    how to use 62-68, 70, 109-110, 114-116

moods of verbs 42

N

narratives

    essays 143-144

    format and features of 137-138

negative contractions 115-116

negative sentences 102

non-count nouns 11, 13, 31

non-defining adjective (relative) clauses 18, 21, 24, 107

not, use of 90

noun clauses 13, 108

noun phrases 13, 103

nouns 4, 10-13, 124, 126, 129, 133

    abstract 12-13, 126

    as adjectives 5, 22

    collective 12, 13, 119

    common 11, 13

    compound 12-13, 124, 126, 129

    count 11, 13, 32

    definition of 4, 10

    examples of types 11-12

generalizing 5, 30, 31

gerunds 12, 13, 43, 124, 126, 129

mass 11, 13, 31

non-count 11, 13, 31

plurals of 10-11

proper 12, 13

qualifying 5, 22, 30

types of 11-12

use of 4, 10-11

O

object of sentence 4, 10, 13, 38-39, 101, 108

ordinary (principal) verbs 38-39

P

parentheses 121

participle phrases 104-105

participles 25, 43, 104-105

    past 25, 38, 49, 51, 54, 56, 57, 61, 69-70, 73-76, 104-105

    perfect 105

    present 25, 48, 51, 53, 56, 57, 61, 104-105

passive verbs 38-39, 69-71, 73-76, 104

    forms 69-71

past participles 25, 38, 49, 51, 54, 56, 57, 61, 69-70, 73-76, 104-105

past tense 44-45, 52-56, 69, 125, 132

    continuous 44, 45, 53, 69

    perfect 44, 45, 54-55, 69

    perfect continuous 44, 45, 56

    simple 44, 45, 52, 69

see also irregular verbs

perfect infinitive 43, 70

perfect participle 105

personal pronouns 14-15

phrasal verbs 44, 106

phrases 103-106

    adjective 23, 103

    adverb 93, 103

    conjunction 97, 103

    definition of 103

    interjection 99, 103

    noun 13, 103

    participle 104-105

    preposition 37, 103

    types of 103-104

    verb 44, 104

plain auxiliary verbs 40-41, 77, 81, 85, 109-110, 114-116

plurals of nouns 10-11

positive sentences 102

possessive adjectives 16, 23, 116

possessive case 4, 10

possessive pronouns 16

predicate of sentence 101

preposition phrases 37, 103

prepositions 6, 34-37, 124, 126-127, 129-130, 134

    definition of 6, 34

    examples 35-37

    types of 34

use of 6, 34

present infinitives 43, 70

present participles 25, 48, 51, 53, 56, 57, 61, 104-105

present tense 46-51, 69, 123, 132

    continuous 44, 45, 48, 58, 69

    perfect 44, 45, 49, 50, 69

    perfect continuous 44, 45, 51

    simple 44, 45, 46-47, 58, 69, 72

    see also irregular verbs

principal verbs 38-39

procedures, format and features of 139

pronoun clauses 21

pronouns 4, 14-21, 124, 127, 130, 134-135

    definition of 4, 14

    demonstrative 19

    emphatic 16-17

    indefinite 20

    interrogative 19

    personal 14-15

    possessive 16

    reflexive 16-17

    relative 18, 21, 24, 107

    types of 14-20

    use of 4, 14

proofreading 136

proper nouns 12, 13

punctuation 117-122

    sentence examples 125, 128, 131, 135

Q

qualifying a noun 5, 30

quantitative adjectives 23

question marks 120

questions

    auxiliary verbs in 109-110

    examples of 110-111

    main types of 109

    positions of adverbs 91

    ways of using 109

quotation marks 120

R

recounts, format and features of 138

reflexive pronouns 16-17

regular verbs 38

relative (adjective) clauses 18, 21, 23-24, 104, 107, 108

relative adverbs 24, 90, 107

relative pronouns 18, 21, 24, 107

reported speech 112-113

reports

    fieldwork 142

    formats and features of 141-143

    general 141

    lab research 141

    research proposal 142-143

responses, format and features of 140

S

semicolons 118-119

sentence adverbs 89, 92

sentences 100-102
    complement of 101
    complex 102
    compound 102
    definition of 100
    length of 100
    negative 102
    object of 4, 10, 38-39, 101
    parts of 101
    positive 102
    predicate of 101
    simple 101
    subject of 4, 10, 101
    types of 101-102

speech
    direct 112-113
    indirect (reported) 112-113

subject of sentence 4, 10, 101

subjunctive mood 42

subordinating conjunctions 96, 97-98, 102, 108

superlative adjectives 23

T

tenses of verbs 44-45, 46-61, 69-71, 123, 125, 128, 132
    using auxiliary verbs 40-41, 49-61, 62-68, 77, 81, 85, 109-110, 114-116
    conditional 44, 59-61, 132
    future 44, 45, 57-58, 128, 132
    past 44, 45, 52-56, 125, 132
    present 44, 45, 46-51, 69, 123, 132
    see also future tense, irregular verbs, past tense, present tense, *to be*, *to have*, *to do*

the (definite article) 5, 30, 31, 33

these and *those* 19, 23

to be, tenses of 77-80

to have, tenses of 81-84

to do, tenses of 85-88

transitive verbs 38-39

U

used to, how to use 67

V

verb phrases 44, 104

verbals 12, 13, 25, 43, 104

verbs 7, 38-88
    active 44, 45, 46-58, 104
    adjectives (with) 5, 22
    auxiliary 40-41, 62-68, 77, 81, 85, 109-110, 114-116
    contractions 114-116
    definition of 7, 38
    forming gerunds 12
    in indirect speech 112-113
    infinitives of 42-43, 70, 73-76
    intransitive 39
    irregular 72-76
    modal 40-41, 62-68, 70, 109, 110, 114-116
    moods of 42
    objects of 4, 10, 13, 38-39, 101, 108

ordinary (principal) 38-39

passive forms 38-39, 69-71, 73-76, 104

phrasal 44, 106

plain auxiliary 40-41, 77, 81, 85, 109-110, 114-116

principal 38-39

regular 38

to be 77-80

to do 85-88

to have 81-84

transitive 38-39

types of 38-41

use of 7, 38

see also auxiliary verbs; irregular verbs; tenses of verbs

W

written language, forms of 137-144

Z

zero conditional 59-61

NOTES

www.ingramcontent.com/pod-product-compliance
Ingram Content Group UK Ltd.
Pitfield, Milton Keynes, MK11 3LW, UK
UKHW051255180426
11947UKWH00020B/1723